Little Treats

whoopie pies, florentines, fudgelicious
gooey chocolate cakes, sticky toffee

Edited by
Catherine Atkinson

foulsham
LONDON • NEW YORK • TORONTO • SYDNEY

foulsham

The Oriel, 33 Bath Road, Slough, Berkshire, SL1 3UF, England

Foulsham books can be found in all good bookshops and direct from www.foulsham.com

ISBN: 978-0-572-03665-2

Contributors' websites:

Alexander M Zhang
Cinara Ferreira
Daniëlle Todd
Eric Fung
Glory Albin
Jaime Leah Davis
Jamieanne Hassler
Jeniffer Paxton
Joe Schrieber
Meeta Wolff
Rita J Lee

Printed in China

Our Menu

Indulgent chocolate

Rich chocolate cake
Soft sponge, drizzled with a luscious chocolate cream sauce, topped with a crisp hazelnut. 8

Choc and walnut brownies
Delicious chewy brownies with a hint of coffee and a crunchy walnut topping. 10

Chocolate explosions
Magnificent chocolate-frosted chocolate cakes with glitzy chocolate decorations. 12

Three-chocolate cheesecake
Milk, plain and white chocolate layers of baked cheesecake top a light sponge base. 14

Choc chip cookie cakes
A frosted and chocolate-chip scattered chocolate cake hides a delicious swirl of cookie dough. 16

Squidgy choconut slices
The perfect pair of chocolate and nuts married in a nut-smothered, melt-in-the-mouth cake. 18

Frivolous cupcakes

Mint surprise cupcakes
A tell-tale twist of peppermint atop the chocolate glaze hints at the surprise inside. 20

Pavlova cupcakes
Raspberries, lychees and a meringue topping rest on a light vanilla sponge softened with cream. 22

Chilli chocolate cupcakes
Aztec-inspired, chilli-spiced chocolate cakes with a chocolate or peanut butter frosting. 24

Ice-cream and toffee cupcakes
Toffee sauce slithers over marshmallow frost as ice-cream hides inside the soft sponge. 26

Earl Grey cupcakes
Subtly flavoured with tea, coated in lemon frosting and finished with candied orange zest. 28

Romantic cupcakes
Buttercream-frosted chocolate cupcakes enhanced with bouquets of sugar-sweet flowers. 30

Under-the-sea cupcakes
Simple, stylish and fun, light-as-air cupcakes make this aquarium of undersea treats. 32

Whoopie pies & crumbly cookies

Choc and cream whoopie pies
Thick whipped cream sandwiches the crunchy-soft cookie layers. 34

Banana whoopie pies
So light, these banana-flavoured, cream-laden pies look as if they could float away. 36

Rose and raspberry macaroons
Fresh raspberries, juicy lychees and rose-scented cream encased in macaroon. 38

Chocolate crinkles
Icing sugar-dusted tops crack away to reveal the delightful, soft, biscuity layers beneath. 40

Chocolate butter cookies
This chocolate and peanut-butter layered treat is a world away from store-bought options. 42

Lemon butter cookies
The tang of fresh lemons infusing real butter shortbread surrounded with a sugar-crystal coating. 44

Toffee chocolate chewies
The treacly flavour of dark sugar permeates these chocolate-chip-dotted toffee biscuits. 46

Snowflake cookies
The perfect winter treat, imaginative designs embellish these delicious sugar-topped biscuits. 48

Chocolate chip cookies
Everyone's favourite, crammed with chocolate chips in a light and luscious base. 50

Gingerbread friends
Timeless and delicious, what better teatime treat than the snap of a crisp ginger biscuit? 52

Bumblebee biscuits
Great for a gift, terrific for a little treat, these fun iced biscuits will just fly off the plate. 54

Cherry coconut florentines
A myriad flavours: melting chocolate, succulent coconut, crunchy nuts, juicy cherries. 56

Honey crunch creams
Orange, honey and walnuts infuse these Greek-inspired biscuits filled with honey-buttercream. 58

Decadent cakes & desserts

Regal toffee cake
Fresh blueberries nestling in shards of sugar caramel crown this buttercream-frosted sponge. 60

Sugar-sweet brownies
The traditional brownie texture made with sweet potato and high-glossed with sugar. 62

Raspberry choc cheesecake
Lemon-hint raspberry cheesecake on butter biscuits drizzled with liqueur-chocolate sauce. 64

Nut and pretzel cheesecake
Soft baked cheesecake and buttered pretzel base split by a hint of melted peanut butter. 66

Sticky toffee puddings
Date-enriched, toffee puddings smothered in caramel sauce and topped with ice-cream. 68

Mint ice-cream and fudge sauce
Peppermint ice-cream is the perfect foil for this gooey chocolate sauce. 70

Mocha brownie puds
Cocoa dusts the glossy chocolate glaze encompassing these impeccable chocolate treats. 72

Fruit and lemon pancakes
Simple elegance: lemon butter, fresh fruits and cream top a sugar-dusted pancake. 74

Tiramisu slice
The Italian treat with everything: rich Mascarpone cheese, soft sponge, chocolate, Marsala, cream. 76

Lemon meringue pie
An old favourite: oven-browned meringue hides a sharp lemon layer and sweet pastry base. 78

Mini chocolate volcanoes
Watch the lava flow of melted truffle ooze from your rich chocolate cake volcano. 80

Scrumptious sweets

Rich chocolate fudge
Rich, dense and oh so chocolatey, this intense fudge is at its best cold from the fridge. 82

Honeycomb cinder toffee
A testament to the magic of cooking: transform sugar and syrup into decadent caramel toffee. 84

Flaked almond toffee
Slender layers of nuts, chocolate and toffee, crisp to bite, satisfying to enjoy. 86

Shortbread and almond bars
A splash of gold leaf sparkles on a chocolate glaze encasing almond-topped shortbread. 88

Cinnamon-sugar doughnuts
Mini size means more cinnamon-sugar coating round light-as-air vanilla doughnuts. 90

Millionaire's shortbread
You'll feel like a million dollars as you bite through the chocolate, caramel and shortbread. 92

Coconut and choc mint bars
Laced with crème de menthe and coconut, crushed crumbs melt into chocolate layers. 94

Go On – Indulge Yourself!

A little treat can lift your spirits in so many ways. It is often just what you need to cheer you up after a lousy day at work or to soften the blow of some bad news. But it's equally good at crowning a celebration or making a good day even better. We know they are naughty … but that makes them so nice!

So here is your collection of sheer indulgence from people who just love baking – from the sweetest fudge to fancy cupcakes, from gooey puddings to crumbly, crunchy cookies. Some are very simple to put together, others need a little more time and attention but every one is worth trying. Make them for yourself or – better still – share them with friends. A gift – however small – that is the result of thought and care is always the most valued. How much better to offer your hostess a unique little box of home-made fudge than a box of chocolates from the supermarket. Wouldn't your grandma prefer some little cakes you've made yourself to a scarf or some more gloves? And nothing says 'I love you' better than a rich, home-made cake oozing chocolate – who cares if it's wonky? – so come on, guys, forget the garage flowers and get baking!

What you need

Everything you need will be found in most kitchens. If you have only a mixing bowl, a wooden spoon, some measuring spoons and a jug, you'll need a little elbow grease to go with them. Or you can use an electric hand mixer or a food processor.
A few other things that will be useful are:

- Cupcake and muffin trays – these help to keep your cakes in shape.

- Baking parchment – this is better than greaseproof (waxed) paper, although that can be used instead.

- Muffin and cake cases – silicone or paper, to keep your cakes nice and neat.

- A sugar thermometer – useful when making sweets, but not essential.

The best ingredients

All the ingredients will be found in your supermarket.

All the various types of sugar have different flavours and slightly different textures, so each recipe will suggest the type that was used to create it. Darker sugars, like muscovado, will give you a more treacly flavour. Anything with a large crystal will not melt so easily into a mixture.

I like to use unsalted (sweet) butter but you can use a spread as long as it is suitable for baking.

For the best results, use chocolate with over 70% cocoa solids – it will say so on the packet. You will pay more for better chocolate but it's worth it.

Skills and techniques

Everything is clearly explained in the recipes so you should be able to follow them without any problems. Here's just a couple of things to remember.

Never forget that when you boil sugar, it gets seriously hot! On no account must you even think about trying it, tasting it or – heaven forbid! – licking the spoon or the bowl when you've just finished.

Chocolate should always be melted gently otherwise it will go grainy and you'll ruin it. The old-fashioned way is to place the broken-up chocolate in a heatproof bowl set over a pan of gently simmering water, stir it occasionally until almost melted, then turn off the heat. Make sure you don't get water in the chocolate. Using oven gloves and being careful of the steam, remove the bowl from the pan and stir until melted.

Alternatively, place the chocolate in a microwave container that will take high temperatures – such as a Pyrex bowl – and microwave on Low in 30-second bursts, stirring in between each one, until almost melted, then keep stirring until melted.

Presenting your gifts

First, think about wrapping your gift so that it remains fresh. Greaseproof (waxed) paper, kitchen foil, clingfilm (plastic wrap) or cellophane are all good options. Then, you need something to protect it from damage: a little box or plastic container perhaps. You may find a pretty box, or you can pop it in a gift bag or wrap it with paper. The finishing touch will be a pretty ribbon to decorate the parcel and tie on your personal message.

Notes on the recipes

- Do not mix metric, imperial and American measures. Follow one set only.
- American terms are given in brackets.
- The ingredients are listed in the order in which they are used in the recipe.
- All spoon measurements are level: 1 tsp = 5 ml; 1 tbsp = 15 ml.
- Eggs are medium unless otherwise stated. If you use a different size, adjust the amount of liquid added to obtain the right consistency.
- Can and packet sizes are approximate and will depend on the particular brand.
- If you substitute a spread of your choice for the butter in the recipes, check that it is suitable for baking.
- All ovens vary, so cooking times have to be approximate. Adjust cooking times and temperatures according to manufacturers' instructions.
- Times indicated are approximate and include preparation and cooking.

1 Indulgent Chocolate

Rich Chocolate Cake

Rita J Lee

Serves 9
Time: 1 hour

For the cake
Butter, softened
    200 g/7 oz/scant 1 cup
Soft light brown sugar
    200 g/7 oz/scant 1 cup
Vanilla extract   10 ml/2 tsp
Large eggs, beaten   4
Self-raising flour   150 g/5 oz/1¼ cups
Cocoa (unsweetened chocolate)
    powder 50 g/2 oz/½ cup
Baking powder   5 ml/1 tsp
Milk   15 ml/1 tbsp

For the sauce
Double (heavy) cream
    250 ml/8 fl oz/1 cup
Plain (semi-sweet) chocolate, chopped
    150 g/5 oz
Blanched hazelnuts (filberts) or walnut
    halves to decorate   9

1 Preheat the oven to 180°C/350ºF/gas 4/fan oven 160ºC. Line a 20 cm/8 in square tin, at least 6 cm/2½ in deep, with baking parchment.

2 To make the cake, cream the butter and sugar until light and fluffy. Add the vanilla and beat again. Add the eggs a little at a time, beating after each addition.

3 Sift in the flour, cocoa and baking powder and fold into the mixture. Add the milk and continue mixing until just blended. Scrape the mixture into the prepared tin and level the top.

4 Bake for 40–45 minutes or until a skewer inserted into the centre comes out clean. Leave to cool in the tin for 10 minutes, then turn out on to a wire rack to cool.

5 To make the sauce, heat the cream in a saucepan until it is steaming hot. Remove from the heat, add the chocolate and whisk until the chocolate has melted.

6 When the cake is cool, or barely warm, cut it into nine squares. Serve with chocolate sauce, either warm or at room temperature, and top each piece with a nut.

Moist and richly chocolatey, what better way to indulge yourself than with a tempting square of this mouth-watering cake, dripping with a spoonful of its gooey chocolate and cream sauce and finished with the flourish of a hazelnut on top.

Choc & Walnut Brownies

Rita J Lee

Makes 9
Time: 40 minutes

Plain (semi-sweet) chocolate,
    chopped   225 g/8 oz
Butter   150 g/5 oz/generous ½ cup
Instant coffee granules   5 ml/1 tsp
Hot water   15 ml/1 tbsp
Eggs, beaten   2
Caster (superfine) sugar
    150 g/5 oz/generous ½ cup
Vanilla extract   5 ml/1 tsp
Self-raising flour   50 g/2 oz/½ cup
Walnut pieces, chopped   100 g/4 oz
Plain chocolate chips
    100 g/4 oz/1 cup
Walnut halves to decorate

1 Preheat the oven to 180ºC/350ºF/gas 4/fan oven 160ºC. Line a 20 cm/8 in square tin, at least 6 cm/2½ in deep, with baking parchment.

2 Melt the chopped chocolate in a heatproof bowl over a pan of barely simmering water, stirring occasionally. Stir in the butter until melted. Remove and leave to cool for a few minutes.

3 Blend together the coffee and water in a large bowl. Add the eggs, sugar and vanilla and whisk together. Gradually add the melted chocolate, then stir in the flour, walnut pieces and chocolate chips.

4 Pour the mixture into the prepared tin. Bake for 30 minutes or until just firm to the touch and a dull sugary crust has formed. Leave to cool in the tin.

5 When completely cold, remove from the tin, cut into nine squares and decorate each with a walnut half.

It's the crunchy top layer combined with a slightly chewy, dense mixture underneath that makes a perfect brownie. Here, you have the addition of chopped walnuts for a real crunch, and just a dash of coffee for a subtle flavour.

Chocolate Explosions

Jeniffer Paxton

Makes 12
Time: 40 minutes

For the cakes
Plain (all-purpose) flour
225 g/8 oz/2 cups
Baking powder 10 ml/2 tsp
Salt 2.5 ml/½ tsp
Cocoa (unsweetened chocolate)
powder 25 g/1 oz/¼ cup
Plain (semi-sweet) chocolate, chopped
150 g/5 oz
Sunflower oil 45 ml/3 tbsp
Egg, beaten 1
Vanilla extract 5 ml/1 tsp
Milk 250 ml/8 fl oz/1 cup

For the whipped chocolate frosting
and truffles
Double (heavy) cream
350 ml/12 fl oz/1½ cups
Unsalted (sweet) butter 15 ml/1 tbsp
Plain chocolate 600 g/1 lb 6 oz
Chocolate or orange liqueur (optional)
30 ml/2 tbsp
Cocoa powder 30 ml/2 tbsp
Plain or white chocolate to decorate

1 Preheat the oven to 180ºC/350ºF/gas 4/ fan oven 160ºC. Line a 12-hole tin with large cake cases (cupcake papers).

2 To make the cakes, sift together the flour, baking powder, salt and cocoa. Melt the chocolate in a heatproof bowl over a pan of barely simmering water, stirring occasionally. Remove the bowl from the heat and stir in the oil, egg and vanilla.

3 Gently fold in the flour mixture alternately with the milk.

4 Divide the mixture between the cake cases and bake for 18–20 minutes or until the centres spring back when gently touched. Cool in the tin for 5 minutes, then transfer to a wire rack to cool.

5 To make the chocolate frosting, put the cream and butter in a saucepan and bring to the boil. Remove from the heat and leave for a minute, then stir in the chocolate until melted. Stir in the liqueur, if using. Leave to cool, then chill.

6 Beat the chocolate mixture until the colour lightens, but do not over-beat or the texture will become grainy. Spoon slightly less than a quarter of the mixture into a small bowl and chill in the fridge. Spoon the rest into a piping bag fitted with a large star nozzle (tip) and pipe generous swirls on the tops of the cakes.

7 Roll tiny balls of the reserved chilled mixture in sifted cocoa powder to make truffles and use to decorate the cakes. Make other decorations by drizzling melted chocolate on to baking parchment and chilling until set. For chocolate curls, run a vegetable peeler down the side of a plain or white chocolate bar. Sprinkle over the frosting before it sets.

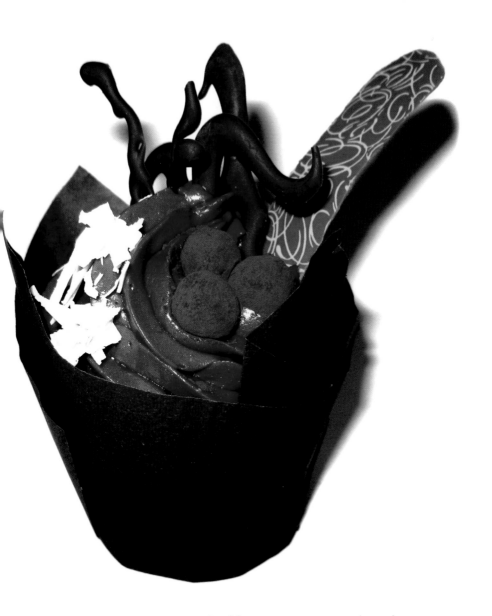

Imagine being presented with your very own chocolate explosion at a dinner party – there's just more, more, more chocolate in this extravagant and beautiful concoction. It's fabulous in every way.

Three-chocolate Cheesecake

Eric Fung

Serves 8–10
Time: 2 hours

For the sponge layers
Eggs, beaten 2
Caster (superfine) sugar
 75 g/3 oz/generous ½ cup
Self-raising flour
 40 g/1½ oz
Cocoa (unsweetened chocolate)
 powder 15 g/½ oz

For the cheesecake layers
Plain (semi-sweet) chocolate, chopped
 100 g/4 oz
White chocolate, chopped 100 g/4 oz
Eggs, separated 3
Caster sugar 100 g/4 oz/½ cup
Full-fat soft cheese, at room
 temperature
 550 g/1¼ lb/2½ cups
Crème fraîche 90 ml/6 tbsp
Vanilla extract 10 ml/2 tsp

1 Preheat the oven to 180ºC/350ºF/gas 4/ fan oven 160ºC. Lightly grease and line a 23 cm/9 in loose-based round cake tin.

2 To make the sponge layers, whisk the eggs and sugar in a bowl until very thick and pale. Fold in the flour and cocoa. Pour into the prepared tin and bake for 20 minutes or until springy. Cool on a wire rack.

3 Clean and re-line the cake tin. Split the cake in half horizontally using a serrated knife. Place one layer in the prepared tin, cut-side up.

4 To make the cheesecake layers, melt the plain chocolate in a heatproof bowl over a pan of barely simmering water, stirring occasionally. Remove the bowl from the heat. Repeat in a separate bowl with the white chocolate.

5 Whisk the egg yolks with half the sugar until pale and thick. Mix together the cheese, crème fraîche and vanilla, then add to the egg mixture and beat until smooth. Mix half of the mixture with the melted plain chocolate and half with the white chocolate.

6 In a separate bowl, whisk the egg whites until stiff. Gradually whisk in the remaining sugar until stiff and glossy. Carefully fold half of this meringue mixture into the plain chocolate mixture. Spoon over the chocolate sponge in the tin and smooth the surface.

7 Carefully place the second chocolate sponge layer on top, cut-side down. Fold the remaining meringue mixture into the white chocolate mixture, spoon on top of the sponge and level the surface.

8 Bake for 50–60 minutes or until the centre is almost firm to the touch. Turn off the oven and leave the cheesecake to cool in the oven with the door ajar.

9 Remove the cheesecake from the tin and serve at room temperature or chilled.

Your version may be as precisely beautiful as this or it may wobble a bit here and there, but it is certain to be a wonderful combination of chocolate flavours, the three layers deliciously complementing each other on your palate.

Choc Chip Cookie Cakes

Jamieanne Hassler

Makes 16
Time: 40 minutes

For the cookies
Butter, softened   50 g/2 oz/¼ cup
Soft light brown sugar
   50 g/2 oz/¼ cup plus 30 ml/2 tbsp
Milk   5 ml/1 tsp
Vanilla extract   5 ml/1 tsp
Plain (all-purpose) flour
   50 g/2 oz/½ cup
Plain (semi-sweet) chocolate chips
   50 g/2 oz/½ cup

For the cakes
Butter, softened   100 g/4 oz/½ cup
Caster (superfine) sugar
   275 g/10 oz/1¼ cups
Eggs   2
Plain flour   75 g/3 oz/¾ cup
Baking powder   5 ml/1 tsp
Salt   a pinch
Cocoa (unsweetened chocolate)
   powder 50 g/2 oz/½ cup
Milk, at room temperature
   120 ml/4 fl oz/½ cup
Vanilla extract   5 ml/1 tsp

For the frosting
Butter, softened   100 g/4 oz/½ cup
Cocoa powder   50 g/2 oz/½ cup
Icing (confectioners') sugar
   500 g/18 oz/3 cups
Milk   30–60 ml/2–4 tbsp
Vanilla extract   5 ml/1 tsp
Chocolate chips to decorate

1 To make the cookie mixture, cream the butter and sugar. Add the milk and vanilla, then sift the flour over and stir until almost mixed. Stir in the chocolate chips. Wrap the dough and chill in the freezer for 30 minutes until firm. Shape into 16 equal balls and chill in the fridge.

2 Preheat the oven to 180ºC/350ºF/gas 4/fan oven 160ºC. Lightly grease two 8-hole cupcake tins or line muffin tins with large cake cases (cupcake papers).

3 To make the cakes, beat the butter until soft, then add the sugar and beat until light and fluffy. Add the eggs, one at a time, beating well after each addition.

4 Gradually add the dry ingredients alternately with the milk and vanilla, folding in gently.

5 Spoon into the prepared tins or cake cases so that they are just over half full. Place a ball of chilled cookie dough in the middle of each.

6 Bake for 20–22 minutes or until just cooked. Leave to cool in the tins for 5 minutes, then transfer to a wire rack to cool.

7 To make the frosting, beat together the butter and cocoa. Sift the icing sugar over a third at a time and stir into the mixture, adding a little milk and vanilla extract with each addition. Beat until light and fluffy. Spoon or pipe the frosting on top of the cakes, then scatter each with a few chocolate chips.

With its swirl of yummy cookie dough lurking deep in the centre of the melting chocolate sponge and topped with a sweet chocolate frosting, who could resist taking a bite of these fun little cakes.

Squidgy Choconut Slices

Rita J Lee

Makes about 20 slices
Time: 25 minutes

Butter   100 g/4 oz/½ cup
Plain (semi-sweet) chocolate, broken
   into pieces   100 g/4 oz/1 cup
Golden (light corn) syrup   15 ml/1 tbsp
Soft light brown sugar
   150 g/5 oz/generous ½ cup
Caster (superfine) sugar
   150 g/5 oz/generous ½ cup
Eggs, beaten   4
Self-raising flour   225 g/8 oz/2 cups
Cocoa (unsweetened chocolate)
   powder   40 g/1½ oz
Mixed nuts, roughly chopped
   100 g/4 oz/1 cup
Plain chocolate chips
   100 g/4 oz/1 cup

1 Preheat the oven to 180ºC/350ºF/gas 4/fan oven 160ºC. Grease and line the base of an 18 x 28 cm/7 x 11 in tin with baking parchment.

2 Melt the butter, broken chocolate and syrup in a heatproof bowl over a pan of barely simmering water, stirring occasionally.

3 Remove from the heat and stir in the sugars. Stir in the eggs, a little at a time, then sift over the flour and cocoa and gently fold in. Spoon into the prepared tin and level the top.

4 Scatter the top evenly with the nuts, followed by the chocolate chips. Bake on the middle shelf of the oven for 25 minutes or until it is risen and firm to the touch.

5 Leave to cool in the tin. Cut into slices and serve slightly warm or cold. Store in an airtight tin.

See photograph on page 7.

2 Frivolous Cupcakes

Mint Surprise Cupcakes

Jeniffer Paxton

Makes 12
Time: 50 minutes

For the cakes
Butter   175 g/6 oz/¾ cup
Mint-flavoured plain (semi-sweet)
  chocolate, chopped   100 g/4 oz
Caster (superfine) sugar
  200 g/7 oz/scant 1 cup
Large eggs, at room temperature   3
Plain (all-purpose) flour
  125 g/4½ oz/generous 1 cup
Cocoa (unsweetened chocolate)
  powder   30 ml/2 tbsp
Baking powder   5 ml/1 tsp

For the mint layer
Butter, at room temperature
  45 ml/3 tbsp
Icing (confectioners') sugar
  250 g/9 oz/1½ cups
Double (heavy) cream or crème fraîche
  20–30 ml/1½–2 tbsp
Peppermint extract   4 ml/¾ tsp
Green food colouring   2–3 drops

For the chocolate ganache
Double cream   120 ml/4 fl oz/½ cup
Plain chocolate, chopped   200 g/7 oz
Golden (corn) syrup (optional)
  5 ml/1 tsp

For the peppermint twist topping
Chewable peppermint lollies or
  sweets   2

1 Preheat the oven to 180°C/350°F/gas 4/ fan oven 160°C. Line a 12-hole muffin or cupcake tin with muffin cases (paper liners).

2 To make the cakes, melt the butter and chocolate in a heatproof bowl over a pan of very hot water, stirring occasionally. Remove the bowl from the pan and leave to cool for 15 minutes.

3 Stir in the sugar, then stir in the eggs, one at a time. Gently fold in the flour, cocoa and baking powder. Do not over-mix.

4 Divide the mixture between the cases and bake for 20 minutes until the cakes look almost cooked, with a slightly indented centre. Transfer the tin to a wire rack to cool for 5 minutes before removing the cakes from the tin to cool completely.

5 To make the mint layer, beat together all the ingredients until smooth. Spread evenly over the cakes, filling the centre hollow. Chill in the fridge for 10 minutes until firm.

6 To make the chocolate ganache, bring the cream to the boil in a small saucepan. Remove from the heat, add the chocolate and stir until smooth. Add the syrup for a softer finish. When cool and thickened, carefully spread over the mint filling.

7 To make the peppermint twist topping, soften the lollies by placing on a plate and microwaving for 10 seconds on Low. Pull off pieces and twist between your fingers, then arrange on top of the cakes.

The swirl of mint on top really gives the game away, so
you know that when you bite through the light, chocolate
cake, you will encounter a wonderfully gooey cave of soft
peppermint in the centre.

Pavlova Cupcakes

Jeniffer Paxton

Makes 12
Time: 40 minutes

For the cakes
Unsalted (sweet) butter, diced
40 g/1½ oz/3 tbsp
Plain (all-purpose) flour
115 g/4½ oz/generous 1 cup
Baking powder   7.5 ml/1½ tsp
Salt   a pinch
Caster (superfine) sugar
150 g/5 oz/generous ½ cup
Full-fat milk   120 ml/4 fl oz/½ cup
Egg   1
Vanilla extract   5 ml/1 tsp

For the mini pavlovas
Egg whites, at room temperature   3
Caster (superfine) sugar
165 g/5½ oz/¾ cup
Cornflour (cornstarch)   10 ml/2 tsp
White vinegar   2.5 ml/½ tsp
Vanilla extract   5 ml/1 tsp

For decorating
Whipping or double (heavy) cream
300 ml/½ pint/1¼ cups
Can of lychees, in syrup, drained
½ x 400 g/14 oz/large
Fresh raspberries   150 g/5 oz
Rose syrup (optional)
15–30 ml/1–2 tbsp

1 Preheat the oven to 160ºC/325ºF/gas 3/ fan oven 145ºC. Line a 12-hole muffin tin with muffin cases (paper liners).

2 To make the cakes, rub the butter into the flour, baking powder and salt until the mixture resembles fine breadcrumbs. Stir in the sugar.

3 Stir in half the milk until just incorporated. Whisk the egg, vanilla and remaining milk together, then add to the bowl and beat for 2 minutes until smooth. Divide the mixture between the cases, filling them about two-thirds full.

4 Bake for 20–25 minutes or until lightly golden and springy to the touch. Leave in the tin for 5 minutes, then transfer to a wire rack to cool. Turn down the oven to 120ºC/250ºF/gas ½/fan oven 110ºC.

5 To make the pavlovas, line a baking (cookie) sheet with baking parchment and, using a glass the size of the cakes, draw 12 circles. Turn the paper over.

6 Whisk the egg whites until soft peaks form, then add the sugar, a spoonful at a time, beating well between each addition, until thick and glossy. Fold in the cornflour, vinegar and vanilla.

7 Spread over the circles to make neat rounds. Bake for 40–45 minutes until firm but still white. Allow to cool in the oven, leaving the door ajar.

8 Lightly whip the cream until soft peaks form and quarter the lychees. Attach each mini pavlova to a cupcake with whipped cream. Top with the remaining whipped cream, raspberries, lychees and a drizzle of rose syrup, if using. Serve straight away.

Stylish and sophisticated, this is classic pavlova meets indulgent cupcake. Perfect for entertaining or when you feel like having a little treat and really spoiling yourself.

Chilli Chocolate Cupcakes

Jamieanne Hassler

Makes 12
Time: 50 minutes

For the cakes
Unsalted (sweet) butter, softened
    100 g/4 oz/½ cup
Caster (superfine) sugar
    275 g/10 oz/1¼ cups
Eggs   2
Plain (all-purpose) flour
    75 g/3 oz/¾ cup
Baking powder   5 ml/1 tsp
Salt   1.5 ml/¼ tsp
Cocoa powder   50 g/2 oz/½ cup
Milk   120 ml/4 fl oz/½ cup
Vanilla extract   5 ml/1 tsp

For the glaze
Double (heavy) cream   90 ml/6 tbsp
Butter   15 ml/1 tbsp
Plain (semi-sweet) chocolate, chopped
    90 g/3½ oz
Chilli powder   5 ml/1 tsp

For the peanut butter frosting
Unsalted butter, softened
    50 g/2 oz/¼ cup
Smooth peanut butter   50 g/2 oz/¼ cup
Icing (confectioners') sugar, sifted
    500 g/18 oz/3 cups
Vanilla extract   5 ml/1 tsp
Milk   30–60 ml/2–4 tbsp
A pinch of cayenne pepper (optional)

For the chocolate buttercream
Butter, softened   100 g/4 oz/½ cup
Cocoa powder   50 g/2 oz/½ cup
Icing sugar   500 g/18 oz/3 cups
Milk   30 ml/2 tbsp
Vanilla extract   5 ml/1 tsp

1 Preheat the oven to 180ºC/350ºF/gas 4/ fan oven 160ºC. Lightly grease or line a 12-hole muffin tin.

2 To make the cakes, beat the butter until soft, then beat in the sugar until light and fluffy. Beat in the eggs one at a time. Fold in the dry ingredients alternately with the milk and vanilla extract.

3 Spoon into the prepared tin so that they are just over half full. Bake for 20 minutes or until well risen and springy to the touch. Cool in the tins for 5 minutes, then on a wire rack.

4 To make the glaze, gently melt the cream and butter in a pan until the cream is starting to bubble around the edges.

5 Put the chocolate and chilli powder in a heatproof bowl, pour over the hot mixture, leave for 30 seconds, then whisk until smooth. Leave to cool, stirring occasionally, until slightly thickened. Spread over the cakes, then leave to set for 15 minutes in a cool place.

6 To make peanut butter frosting, beat the butter, peanut butter, icing sugar, vanilla and 30 ml/2 tbsp of the milk until fluffy, adding more milk if necessary.

7 To make chocolate buttercream, beat all the ingredients until smooth, adding extra milk if necessary.

8 Spoon your chosen frosting into a piping bag with a large star nozzle and pipe swirls on top of the cakes. If liked, sprinkle the peanut butter frosting with a dash of cayenne pepper.

Spicing chocolate with chilli is a Central and South American trick that really brings out the flavours. You just need to make sure you use a 'pure' chilli powder, without other added spices and flavourings, to get the best results.

Ice-cream & Toffee Cupcakes

Jamieanne Hassler

Makes 12
Time: 40 minutes +
1 hour freezing

For the cakes
Butter, softened   100 g/4 oz/½ cup
Soft light brown sugar
   100 g/4 oz/½ cup
Eggs, beaten   2
Self-raising flour   75 g/3 oz/¾ cup
Cocoa (unsweetened chocolate)
   powder   25 g/1 oz/¼ cup
Milk   10 ml/2 tsp
Good-quality ice-cream
   600 ml/1 pint/2½ cups

For the toffee sauce
Unsalted (sweet) butter
   25 g/1 oz/2 tbsp
Soft dark brown sugar
   75 g/3 oz/¼ cup
Double (heavy) cream
   150 ml/¼ pint/¾ cup

For the marshmallow frosting
Egg white   1
Caster (superfine) sugar
   175 g/6 oz/¾ cup
Warm water   30 ml/2 tbsp
Golden (light corn) syrup   5 ml/1 tsp
Vanilla extract   2.5 ml/½ tsp
White marshmallows, snipped into
   small pieces   50 g/2 oz
Chocolate chips   50 g/2 oz/½ cup

1 Preheat the oven to 180ºC/350ºF/gas 4/ fan oven 160ºC. Line a 12-hole cupcake tin with muffin cases (paper liners).

2 To make the cakes, beat the butter and sugar until creamy. Add the eggs, then sift the flour and cocoa over. Add the milk, then beat until smooth.

3 Divide the mixture between the cake cases, filling about three-quarters full. Bake for 15 minutes until risen and firm. Leave them in the tins for a few minutes, then transfer to a wire rack to cool.

4 Freeze the cakes for 30 minutes to firm them. Remove and reserve the paper cases. Slice each cake in half horizontally. Spread 15–30 ml/1–2 tbsp of softened ice-cream on the bottom half of each cupcake, then replace the top. Place the cupcakes back into the cases, put them in the muffin tin and return to the freezer for at least 1 hour. Meanwhile, make the toppings.

5 To make toffee sauce, gently melt the butter and sugar in a pan, stirring. Stir in the cream and simmer for 2 minutes until smooth. Set aside to cool a little.

6 To make marshmallow frosting, put the egg white, sugar, water and syrup in a heatproof bowl over a pan of boiling water. Beat for about 7 minutes until the mixture stands in peaks. Add the vanilla and marshmallows and whisk gently until the marshmallows have melted. Remove the bowl from the heat and cool for 2–3 minutes.

7 Remove the cakes from the paper linings and spread the frosting on top. Drizzle with the warm toffee sauce and sprinkle with the chocolate chips.

Ice-cream, chocolate, cream and toffee – all in this one amazing little treat. Take a moment to watch the rich toffee sauce slowly slide down the side of the cake before you sink your teeth into its soft centre.

Earl Grey Cupcakes

Jeniffer Paxton

Makes 12
Time: 40 minutes

For the cakes
Earl Grey tea bags   2
Plain (all-purpose) flour
    175 g/6 oz/1½ cups
Baking powder   5 ml/1 tsp
Caster (superfine) sugar
    275 g/10 oz/1¼ cups
Butter, softened   100 g/4 oz/½ cup
Orange zest, finely grated   ½ orange
Eggs, beaten   3
Milk   175 ml/6 fl oz/¾ cup

For the candied orange zest
Orange zest, cut into strips   2 oranges
Caster (superfine) sugar
    100 g/4 oz/1 cup
Water   175 ml/6 fl oz/¾ cup

For the lemon frosting
Icing (confectioners') sugar
    75 g/3 oz/½ cup
Butter, softened   75 g/3 oz/6 tbsp
**Full-fat soft cheese, at room
    temperature**   175 g/6 oz/¾ cup
Lemon zest, finely grated   1 lemon
Lemon juice   5 ml/1 tsp

1 Preheat the oven to 180ºC/350ºF/gas 4/ fan oven 160ºC. Line a 12-hole muffin tin with large cupcake or muffin cases (paper liners).

2 To make the cakes, grind the contents of the tea bags in a spice grinder or with a pestle and mortar until fine, then sift into a bowl with the flour and baking powder, discarding any larger pieces left in the sieve (strainer).

3 Put the sugar, butter and orange zest in another bowl and beat until smooth and creamy. Add the eggs, one at a time, beating well after each addition.

4 Mix in the flour mixture and milk alternately, starting and finishing with the flour mixture. Do not over-beat.

5 Divide the mixture between the cake cases. Bake for 18–22 minutes or until golden and springy. Leave in the tin for a few minutes, then transfer to a wire rack to cool.

6 While the cakes are cooking, make the candied orange zest. Bring the zest, sugar and water to the boil in a small saucepan, then reduce the heat to low and simmer until the zest is translucent. Turn off the heat and leave to cool in the syrup.

7 To make the lemon frosting, beat the icing sugar and butter until smooth, then beat in the cheese. Finally, beat in the lemon zest and juice.

8 Ice the cakes with the lemon frosting, then top with candied orange zest and a little of the syrup.

The subtle flavours of this aristocratic blend are gently infused
into this lightly orange-flavoured cake, which is then
topped with lemon frosting and finished with fine strips of
candied orange zest.

Romantic Cupcakes

Glory Albin

Makes 24
Time: 50 minutes

For the cakes
Plain (all-purpose) flour
200 g/7 oz/1¾ cups
Cocoa (unsweetened chocolate)
powder   75 g/3 oz/¾ cup
Baking powder   7.5 ml/1½ tsp
Bicarbonate of soda (baking soda)
7.5 ml/1½ tsp
Salt   5 ml/1 tsp
Caster (superfine) sugar
225 g/8 oz/1 cup
Eggs, beaten   3
Full-fat milk   250 ml/8 fl oz/1 cup
Sunflower oil   120 ml/4 fl oz/½ cup
Vanilla extract   10 ml/2 tsp
Boiling water   250 ml/8 fl oz/1 cup

For the frosting
Butter, softened   100 g/4 oz/½ cup
Cream cheese, at room temperature
225 g/8 oz/1 cup
Vanilla extract   5 ml/1 tsp
Cocoa powder   50 g/2 oz/½ cup
Icing (confectioner's) sugar
700 g/1½ lb/4 cups
Double (heavy) cream or milk
15–30 ml/1–2 tbsp
Coloured sugar paste flowers and
butterflies and sugar balls or
sprinkles to decorate

1 Preheat the oven to 180ºC/350ºF/gas 4/ fan oven 160ºC. Line two 12-hole muffin tins with large cupcake or muffin cases (paper liners).

2 To make the cakes, sift the flour, cocoa, baking powder, bicarbonate of soda and salt into a large bowl. Stir in the sugar.

3 Make a hollow in the middle and add the eggs, milk, oil and vanilla. Beat until smooth and creamy. Stir in the boiling water.

4 Divide the mixture between the cake cases, filling about two-thirds full. Bake for 22–24 minutes or until well risen and springy to the touch. Leave in the tin for 5 minutes, then transfer to a wire rack to cool.

5 To make the frosting, beat the butter until creamy. Add the cheese and beat until combined and smooth. Beat in the vanilla.

6 Sift the cocoa and icing sugar over and stir until mixed, then beat for a minute or two. Stir in enough of the cream or milk to make a soft piping consistency. Continue beating until light and fluffy.

7 Spoon the frosting into a piping bag fitted with a large star nozzle (tip) and pipe generous swirls on top of the cakes (or spread the icing on the top if you prefer). Decorate with sugar paste flowers and butterflies and sugar balls or sprinkles.

Taking the time to bake something special for someone you love really shows how much you care. It might be a romantic gesture to your partner or a thank-you to your mum, but these delicious cupcakes with their colourful bouquets are sure to please.

Under-the-sea Cupcakes

Gabriela Cacheux

Makes 12
Time: 50 minutes

For the cakes
Butter   225 g/8 oz/1 cup
Caster (superfine) sugar
   225 g/8 oz/1 cup
Eggs, beaten   4
Self-raising flour   225 g/8 oz/2 cups
Milk   15 ml/1 tbsp
Vanilla extract   5 ml/1 tsp

For the icing (frosting)
Apricot jam (conserve)   90 ml/6 tbsp
Brandy or water   15 ml/1 tbsp
White sugar paste (ready-to-roll icing)
   450 g/1 lb
Icing (confectioners') sugar for dusting
Food colouring pastes

1 Preheat the oven to 180ºC/350ºF/gas 4/ fan oven 160ºC. Line a 12-hole muffin or cupcake tin with muffin cases (paper liners).

2 To make the cakes, put the butter and sugar in a bowl and beat until light and fluffy. Add the eggs, a little at a time, beating well after each addition and adding a little of the flour if the mixture begins to curdle.

3 Sift the flour over the creamed mixture. Mix together the milk and vanilla and add to the bowl. Gently fold everything together. Divide between the cake cases.

4 Bake in the oven for about 15 minutes or until golden-brown, well-risen and firm to the touch. Leave in the tins for 5 minutes, then transfer to a wire rack.

5 When the cakes are cool, to make the icing put the jam in a pan with the brandy or water. Heat until bubbling, stirring occasionally, then sieve (strain) the jam. Brush over the tops of the cakes in a thin, even layer.

6 Roll out two-thirds of the sugar paste on a surface lightly dusted with icing sugar and cut out rounds the same size as the tops of the cakes. Place one on top of each, pressing gently and smoothing.

7 Colour the remaining sugar paste several different colours (use the scraps of rolled out sugar paste as well) and use to make sea, fish, seaweed and flower decorations. Attach to the cakes with a very light brushing of water. Leave to dry for a few hours, then store in an airtight container.

See photograph on page 6.

3 Whoopie Pies & Crumbly Cookies

Choc & Cream Whoopie Pies

Alexander M Zhang

Makes about 12
Time: 30 minutes

For the sponges
Butter   75 g/3 oz/⅓ cup
Large egg   1
Caster (superfine) sugar
    150 g/5 oz/generous ½ cup
Soured (dairy sour) cream, at room
    temperature   150 ml/¼ pint/⅔ cup
Vanilla extract   10 ml/2 tsp
Milk   30 ml/2 tbsp
Plain (all-purpose) flour
    225 g/8 oz/2 cups
Cocoa (unsweetened chocolate)
    powder   50 g/2 oz/½ cup
Bicarbonate of soda (baking soda)
    4 ml/¾ tsp

For the filling
Whipping or double (heavy) cream
    300 ml/½ pint/1¼ cups
Icing (confectioners') sugar
    60 ml/4 tbsp, plus extra for dusting

1 Preheat the oven to 160ºC/325ºF/gas 3/ fan oven 145ºC. Line two baking (cookie) sheets with baking parchment.

2 To make the sponges, melt the butter in a small saucepan over a low heat. Leave to cool for a few minutes. Put the egg and sugar in a bowl and beat for 2–3 minutes with an electric whisk until light and fluffy.

3 Pour in the melted butter, soured cream, vanilla and milk. Gently fold into the mixture. Sift the flour, cocoa and bicarbonate of soda over. Gently fold everything together.

4 Scoop heaped teaspoonfuls of the mixture on to the baking sheets, making sure they are well spaced; you should have about 24 in total. Bake for 10–12 minutes until just firm. Leave on the baking sheets for five minutes, then transfer to a wire rack to cool.

5 To make the filling, pour the cream into a bowl and whisk for about 2 minutes until just beginning to thicken. Sift the icing sugar over, then whisk again until soft peaks form.

6 Spoon and spread the cream over the flat sides of half of the sponges, then top each with a second sponge. Lightly dust the tops with icing sugar.

The wonderful whipped cream filling is the perfect colour contrast to the dark chocolate whoopie pie – but just wait until you can taste the texture and flavour contrast on your tongue. It's the perfect little treat.

Banana Whoopie Pies

Jamieanne Hassler

Makes about 18
Time: 30 minutes

For the sponges
Plain (all-purpose) flour
100 g/4 oz/1 cup
Baking powder   1.5 ml/¼ tsp
Bicarbonate of soda (baking soda)
1.5 ml/¼ tsp
Salt   1.5 ml/¼ tsp
Ripe banana   ½
Soured (dairy sour) cream
60 ml/4 tbsp
Vanilla extract   2.5 ml/½ tsp
Unsalted (sweet) butter, softened
65 g/2½ oz/4 tbsp
Granulated sugar   50 g/2 oz/¼ cup
Soft light brown sugar
50 g/2 oz/¼ cup
Small egg, beaten   1

For the filling
Full-fat soft cheese   225 g/8 oz/1 cup
Vanilla extract   2.5 ml/½ tsp
Icing (confectioners') sugar
75 g/3 oz/½ cup, plus extra for
dusting

1 Preheat the oven to 180ºC/350ºF/gas 4/
fan oven 160ºC. Line two baking (cookie)
sheets with baking parchment.

2 Sift the flour, baking powder, bicarbonate
of soda and salt into a bowl.

3 Mash the banana to a smooth purée in
a small bowl. Stir in the soured cream
and vanilla extract.

4 Beat the butter in a bowl until soft
and creamy. Add the sugars and beat
together until light. Gradually add the
egg, beating well after each addition.

5 Add about a third of the flour mixture
and fold into the butter mixture until
almost mixed, then add half the banana
mixture and stir in. Continue adding the
flour and banana mixture, ending with
the flour mixture. Mix together until just
combined.

6 Spoon into a piping bag fitted with a
large plain nozzle (tip). Pipe 3 cm/
1¼ in rounds on to the baking tray.
Alternatively, place spoonfuls of the
mixture on to the sheets rather than
piping.

7 Bake for 10–12 minutes or until lightly
golden and springy. Transfer the sponges,
still on the sheets, to wire racks to cool.

8 To make the filling, beat together the
cheese and vanilla. Sift the icing sugar
over and stir until combined.

9 Spoon and spread the filling over the flat
sides of half of the sponges, then top
each with a second sponge. Lightly dust
the tops with icing sugar.

Just look at these cute little whoopie pies tempting you to pop them into your mouth so you can enjoy that distinctive banana flavour that brings all those wonderful childhood memories flooding back.

Rose & Raspberry Macaroons

Grace Chan

Makes 12
Time: 45 minutes

For the macaroons
Egg whites   2
Cream of tartar   a pinch
Pink food colouring   2 drops
Icing (confectioners') sugar, sifted
    100 g/4 oz/²⁄₃ cup
Caster (superfine) sugar
    25 g/1 oz/2 tbsp
Ground almonds   100 g/4 oz/1 cup

For the filling
Double (heavy) cream
    150 ml/¼ pint/²⁄₃ cup
Rose water   10 ml/2 tsp
Can of lychees in syrup, drained
    400 g/14 oz/large
Fresh raspberries   150 g/5oz

1 Line two baking (cookie) sheets with baking parchment. To make the macaroons, whisk the egg whites with an electric whisk until they are foamy. Add the cream of tartar, food colouring and a heaped tablespoonful of icing sugar and carry on whisking until fairly thick.

2 Add the remaining icing sugar, a heaped tablespoonful at a time, whisking for a few seconds after each addition, until the egg whites are in stiff peaks when the whisk is lifted. Add the caster sugar and ground almonds and gently fold into the mixture.

3 Spoon into a piping bag with a large plain nozzle (tip) and pipe 24 6 cm/2½ in rounds on to the baking sheets. Alternatively, scoop heaped teaspoonfuls of the mixture then, using the back of the spoon, gently smooth into rounds. Leave to stand for 30 minutes (this helps prevent them cracking during cooking).

4 Preheat the oven to 110ºC/225ºF/gas ¼/fan oven 100ºC. Bake the macaroons for 30 minutes. Turn off the oven and leave for a further 30 minutes, then take them out of the oven and leave on the trays to cool.

5 To make the filling, pour the cream into a bowl. Add the rose water, then whisk until thick and soft peaks form. Pat the lychees dry on kitchen paper (paper towels).

6 Place a heaped teaspoonful of rose cream in the middle of one of the macaroons, then arrange raspberries and lychees around the edges. Place a second macaroon on top. Serve straight away.

The subtle crunch of almond macaroons that touch your tongue then begins to melt and mingle with the fresh raspberries, lychees and rose-scented cream – what better way to give yourself a little treat?

Chocolate Crinkles

Jamieanne Hassler

Makes about 20
Time: 30 minutes

Plain (semi-sweet) chocolate, chopped
    200 g/7 oz
Butter   50 g/2 oz/¼ cup
Caster (superfine) sugar
    125 g/4½ oz/generous ½ cup
Eggs   3
Vanilla extract   5 ml/1 tsp
Plain (all-purpose) flour
    175 g/6 oz/1½ cups
Cocoa (unsweetened chocolate)
    powder   25 g/1 oz/¼ cup
Baking powder   2.5 ml/½ tsp
Icing (confectioners') sugar
    100 g/4 oz/¾ cup

1 Put the chocolate and butter in a heatproof bowl over a pan of barely simmering water and stir occasionally until melted. Remove from the heat and stir in the caster sugar. Continue stirring until the sugar has melted.

2 Add the eggs, one at a time, beating well after each addition. Stir in the vanilla.

3 Sift the flour, cocoa and baking powder over the melted mixture and gently stir until just mixed. Cover and chill for 1 hour or until the mixture is firm.

4 Preheat the oven to160°C/325°F/gas 3/ fan oven 145°C. Line two baking (cookie) sheets with non-stick baking parchment.

5 Sift the icing sugar into a bowl. Using a teaspoon, scoop up the dough and roll into small balls between the palms of your hands. Drop them one at a time into the icing sugar and roll until thoroughly coated.

6 Place the balls spaced well apart on the baking sheets, pressing them down very slightly to prevent them rolling off. Bake for 12–15 minutes.

7 Leave to cool on the baking sheets for 5 minutes, then transfer to a wire rack to cool. Store in an airtight container and eat within 3 days.

Half way from a cookie to a tiny cake, simple enough to make for yourself any time but impressive enough to serve to friends, you'll soon find this great little recipe will become one of your favourite treats.

Chocolate Butter Cookies

Cinara Ferreira

Makes about 24
Time: 25 minutes

Butter   100 g/4 oz/½ cup
Caster (superfine) sugar
    100 g/4 oz/½ cup
Soft light brown sugar
    65 g/2½ oz/⅓ cup
Large egg, beaten   1
Vanilla extract   2.5 ml/½ tsp
Plain (all-purpose) flour
    225 g/8 oz/2 cups
Cocoa (unsweetened chocolate)
    powder   40 g/1½ oz/⅓ cup
Baking powder   2.5 ml/½ tsp
Salt   1.5 ml/¼ tsp
Peanut butter chips   175g/6 oz/¾ cup

1 Preheat the oven to 180ºC/350ºF/gas 4/ fan oven 160ºC. Line two baking (cookie) sheets with baking parchment.

2 Cream the butter and sugars together in a large bowl until fluffy. Gradually beat in the egg, a little at a time, beating well after each addition. Stir in the vanilla.

3 Sift the flour, cocoa, baking powder and salt over the creamed mixture. Add the peanut butter chips, then gently stir everything together.

4 Drop rounded tablespoonfuls of the mixture on to the baking sheets, spacing them well apart.

5 Bake for 9–11 minutes or until the cookies are set at the edges and the tops are slightly cracked. Leave to cool on the baking sheets for 5 minutes, then transfer to a wire rack to cool. Store in an airtight container.

The combination of chocolate and peanut butter is such a favourite that our collection of little treats would not be complete without this delectable rich chocolate cookie enhanced with a light sprinkling of salty-sweet peanut butter.

Lemon Butter Cookies

Daniëlle Todd

Makes about 25
Time: 30 minutes

Unsalted (sweet) butter, softened
    100 g/4 oz/½ cup
Icing (confectioners') sugar, sifted
    50 g/2 oz/⅓ cup
Large egg yolk, at room
    temperature   1
Salt   a pinch
Vanilla extract   5 ml/1 tsp
Lemon zest, finely grated
    1 small lemon
Plain (all-purpose) flour
    100 g/4 oz/1 cup
Granulated sugar   100 g/4 oz/½ cup

1 Put the butter in a bowl and beat for a few seconds until creamy. Add the icing sugar a third at a time, beating between each addition until smooth.

2 Add half the egg yolk, the salt, vanilla and lemon zest and beat until blended. Sift the flour over and gently stir into the mixture. Gather the dough into a ball and knead for just a few seconds until smooth. Wrap in clingfim (plastic wrap) and chill in the fridge for 30 minutes.

3 Using your hands, roll the dough into a log-shape about 3 cm/1¼ in thick. Re-wrap in cling film and chill in the fridge for 2 hours.

4 Preheat the oven to 180ºC/350ºF/gas 4/fan oven 160ºC and line two baking (cookie) sheets with baking parchment.

5 Spread out the granulated sugar on a piece of baking parchment. Whisk the reserved egg yolk in a small bowl, then brush lightly over the sides of the dough log. Roll in the sugar until evenly coated all over.

6 Using a sharp knife, slice the log into cookies about 5mm/¼ in thick. Place on the lined baking sheets, spacing them well apart.

7 Bake for 12–14 minutes or until the cookies are firm but not browned (it's fine if the egg-glazed edges brown a little). Leave on the baking sheets for 5 minutes, then transfer to a wire rack to cool. Store in an airtight container.

Shortbread with a delightful difference, these superb circles are flavoured with fresh lemons to give a little zest to your sweet treat, plus there's the added crunch of the sugar crystals to make them even more moreish.

Toffee Chocolate Chewies

Jaime Leah Davis

Makes about 30
Time: 25 minutes

Unsalted (sweet) butter
225 g/8 oz/1 cup
Soft dark brown sugar
225 g/8 oz/1 cup
Caster (superfine) sugar
225 g/8 oz/1 cup
Vanilla extract   10 ml/2 tsp
Large egg   1
Large egg yolk   1
Strong white bread flour
225 g/8 oz/2 cups
Bicarbonate of soda (baking soda)
5 ml/1 tsp
Salt   2.5–5 ml/½–1 tsp
Plain (semi-sweet) chocolate chips
75 g/3 oz/¾ cup
Chopped soft toffees   75 g/3 oz/¾ cup

1 Heat the butter over a low heat until melted. Pour into a bowl, add the sugars and beat until smooth and combined. Stir in the vanilla, the egg and the egg yolk.

2 Sift the flour, bicarbonate of soda and salt into a bowl. Add to the butter and sugar mixture a third at a time, stirring until almost mixed. Stir in the chocolate chips and toffee pieces until combined.

3 Cover and chill the mixture in the fridge for at least 2 hours, and for up to 36 hours, until firm.

4 Preheat the oven to 160ºC/325ºF/gas 3/fan oven 145ºC and line two baking (cookie) sheets with baking parchment.

5 Scoop up tablespoonfuls of the dough and roll into balls. Place on the baking sheets, spacing about 5 cm/2 in apart. Bake for 11–12 minutes or, if you prefer a crisper cookie, for up to 15 minutes.

6 Allow the cookies to cool on the baking sheets, then transfer to a wire rack lined with kitchen paper (paper towels). When cold, store in an airtight tin.

Cookies at their chewiest, these unassuming little treats may look slender but they are big on flavour, combining the treacly flavour of dark brown sugar with traditional toffee dotted with chocolate chips.

Snowflake Cookies

Glory Albin

Makes about 35
Time: 30 minutes

For the cookies
Unsalted (sweet) butter, softened
225 g/8 oz/1 cup
Caster (superfine) sugar
225 g/8 oz/1 cup
Large egg, beaten 1
Vanilla extract 5 ml/1 tsp
Plain (all-purpose) flour
300 g/11 oz/2¾ cups,
plus extra for dusting
Baking powder 5 ml/1 tsp

For icing (frosting) and decorating
Egg white 1
Icing (confectioners') sugar, sifted
225 g/8 oz/1⅓ cups, plus extra for
dusting
Blue food colouring
White sugar paste (ready-to-roll
icing) 500 g/18 oz
Caster sugar 15–30 ml/1–2 tbsp
Edible silver balls

1 To make the cookies, cream the butter
and sugar until light and fluffy. Add the
egg a little at time, beating after each
addition, then beat in the vanilla.

2 Sift in the flour and baking powder and
mix to a dough. Lightly knead on a
floured surface for a few seconds until
smooth. Cut in half, flatten each piece
slightly, then wrap in clingfilm (plastic
wrap) and chill in the fridge for 2 hours
or in the freezer for 20–30 minutes.

3 Roll out one piece of dough at a time
on a lightly floured surface until about
5 mm/¼ in thick. Cut out snowflake
shapes with cookie cutters and transfer
to ungreased baking (cookie) sheets.

4 Put the baking sheets in the freezer for
about 5 minutes. Preheat the oven to
180ºC/350ºF/gas 4/fan oven 160ºC.

5 Bake the cookies for 8–10 minutes
until very lightly browned. Leave on
the baking sheets for 5 minutes, then
transfer to a wire rack to cool.

6 To make icing, lightly whisk the egg
white for a few seconds. Using a
wooden spoon, stir in the icing sugar a
heaped tablespoonful at a time until the
mixture is thick and stands in stiff peaks.

7 Spoon half the royal icing into another
bowl and stir in 1–2 drops of blue food
colouring. Cover with clingfilm.

8 If liked, colour some of the sugar paste a
pale blue colour, or leave it all white. Roll
out the sugar paste thinly on a surface
lightly dusted with icing sugar. Cut out
snowflake shapes with the cookie cutters
and place on top of the cookies.

9 Spoon the white and blue royal icing
into piping bags fitted with small plain
nozzles (tips). Pipe snowflake designs on
top of the sugar paste-covered cookies.
Sprinkle a little caster sugar over and
place a few silver balls on some of the
patterns immediately after piping.

10 Let the icing dry, then pack the cookies,
interleaving the layers with baking
parchment, in an airtight container.

You'll need some cookie cutters to make these festive cookies – or you can adapt the recipe to make your own shapes and designs. And if you don't have cookie cutters, just improvise with a cardboard template and a knife.

Chocolate Chip Cookies

Anne McDonagh

Makes about 24
Time: 25 minutes

Butter, softened   75 g/3 oz/⅓ cup
Caster (superfine) sugar
      75 g/3 oz/⅓ cup
Soft light brown sugar
      75 g/3 oz/⅓ cup
Egg, beaten   1
Vanilla extract   5 ml/1 tsp
Plain (all-purpose) flour
      175 g/6 oz/1½ cups
Baking powder   2.5 ml/½ tsp
Plain (semi-sweet) chocolate chips
      100 g/4 oz/1 cup

1 Preheat the oven to 180ºC/350ºF/gas 4/ fan oven 160ºC. Line two baking (cookie) sheets with baking parchment.

2 Put the butter and sugars in a large bowl and beat with a wooden spoon until smooth and creamy. Beat in the egg, a little at a time, then stir in the vanilla.

3 Sift the flour and baking powder into the bowl. Gently stir until almost mixed, then add the chocolate chips and continue stirring until combined.

4 Put heaped teaspoonfuls of the mixture on to the baking trays, spacing them slightly apart. Flatten slightly with the back of the fork.

5 Bake for 10 minutes or until firm and golden brown. Leave on the baking sheets for a few minutes, then transfer to a wire rack to cool. When cold, store in an airtight container.

Everyone's childhood favourite, this is the best version of
the best cookie – so easy to make, you can give yourself a
little treat at a moment's notice. A cup of morning coffee or
afternoon tea is just waiting for one of these to make it perfect.

Gingerbread Friends

Fiona Skerrett

Makes 20–25
Time: 25 minutes

Plain (all-purpose) flour, plus extra for
    dusting   350 g/12 oz/3 cups
Ground ginger   10 ml/2 tsp
Ground cinnamon   5 ml/1 tsp
Bicarbonate of soda (baking soda)
    5 ml/1 tsp
Chilled butter, cut into small pieces
    100 g/4 oz/½ cup
Dark muscovado sugar
    175 g/6 oz/¾ cup
Egg   1
Golden (light corn) syrup
    30 ml/2 tbsp
Tubes of writing icing or royal icing
    (see page 48), to decorate

1 Preheat the oven to 180ºC/350ºF/gas 4/
fan oven 160ºC. Line two baking (cookie)
sheets with baking parchment.

2 Sift the flour, ginger, cinnamon and
bicarbonate of soda into a bowl. Rub
the butter into the flour until the mixture
resembles fine breadcrumbs. Stir in the
sugar, breaking up any lumps with your
fingers.

3 Beat together the egg and syrup. Add
to the flour mixture and stir everything
together to make a dough. Knead the
dough on a lightly floured surface for a
few seconds until smooth.

4 Cut the dough in half and wrap one
piece in clingfilm (plastic wrap). Roll out
the other piece until the dough is about
5 mm/¼ in thick.

5 Use gingerbread cutters to cut out
gingerbread people. Carefully transfer
to the baking sheets. Repeat with the
second piece of dough.

6 Bake for 12–15 minutes until slightly
darker in colour. Leave on the baking
sheets for 5 minutes, then transfer to a
wire rack to cool.

7 Pipe on faces and clothing details with
writing icing or royal icing to create
individual gingerbread people. When the
icing is dry, store in an airtight container.

These fun little treats are guaranteed to bring a smile to the face of anyone who sees them – and that's reason enough to get baking. And if you need another reason, just think how much you'll smile when you eat them.

Bumblebee Biscuits

Maysem Hammad

Makes about 12
Time: 25 minutes

For the biscuits
Butter, softened   75 g/3 oz/$\frac{1}{3}$ cup
Icing (confectioner's) sugar   25 g/1 oz
Plain (all-purpose) flour
　　100 g/4 oz/1 cup,
　　plus extra for dusting

To decorate
Yellow sugar paste (ready-to-roll icing)
　　175 g/6 oz
White sugar paste   100 g/4 oz
Black sugar paste   100 g/4 oz
Pink sugar paste   25 g/1 oz
Icing sugar, sifted
　　60 ml/4 tbsp, plus extra for dusting
Hot water   5 ml/1 tsp

1 To make the biscuits, put the butter in a bowl and beat for a few seconds until creamy. Sift the icing sugar over and stir in until the mixture is smooth.

2 Sift the flour over and stir it in, then squeeze the dough together and knead for just a few seconds on a lightly floured surface. Wrap the dough in clingfilm (plastic wrap) and chill in the fridge for 30 minutes.

3 Preheat the oven to 180ºC/350ºF/gas 4/ fan oven 160ºC. Line two baking (cookie) sheets with baking parchment.

4 Roll out the dough until it is about 4 mm/$\frac{1}{6}$ in thick. Using a cutter or cardboard stencil, cut out bee shapes, each about 7.5 cm/3 in. Carefully transfer them to the baking sheets.

5 Bake for 10–12 minutes or until the biscuits are a light golden-brown colour. Leave on the tray for a few minutes, then transfer to a wire rack to cool.

6 To decorate, roll out the coloured sugar paste on a surface lightly dusted with icing sugar and cut out shapes to represent the body, wings, eyes and cheeks of the bees.

7 Blend together the icing sugar and water. One at a time, very lightly brush the back of the shapes with the glaze, then attach the sugar paste to the biscuits. Leave to harden and set for an hour or two, then store in an airtight container.

A simple little shortbread-style cookie, these make great gifts and party treats, but you don't need to wait for a party! They taste delicious with a hot drink, or you can serve them with ice-cream for dessert.

Cherry Coconut Florentines

Amy Davies

Makes about 12
Time: 25 minutes

Butter   75 g/3 oz/6 tbsp
Caster (superfine) sugar   75 ml/5 tbsp
Plain (all-purpose) flour   45 ml/3 tbsp
Flaked (slivered) almonds
   50 g/2 oz/½ cup
Glace (candied) cherries, chopped
   50 g/2 oz/¼ cup
Desiccated (shredded) coconut
   50 g/2 oz/½ cup
White chocolate chips
   75 g/3 oz/¾ cup
Plain (semi-sweet) chocolate chips
   75 g/3 oz/¾ cup

1 Preheat the oven to 180ºC/350ºF/gas 4/ fan oven 160ºC. Line a large baking tray with baking parchment.

2 Gently heat the butter and sugar in a heavy-based pan over a low heat, stirring occasionally, until the sugar has melted. Stir in the flour, almonds, cherries and coconut.

3 Roughly spread the florentine mixture in a thin layer on the baking tray; don't worry if you have a few small gaps as the mixture will melt together in the oven. Bake for 10–12 minutes or until a rich golden colour.

4 Remove from the oven and leave to cool for a minute or two, then scatter the chocolate chips evenly over the top – the white chocolate chips at one end and the plain at the other. Leave for 2 minutes until melted, then spread the chocolate evenly (the stars that will be cut from the middle will have a mixture of both plain and white chocolate toppings).

5 Leave to cool. When the chocolate has completely set, stamp out stars with a 6 cm/2½ in cutter. Cut them out close together so that there are minimal trimmings. Store in a single layer on baking parchment in an airtight container.

These star-shaped fruity, nutty florentines make ideal treats for Christmas and other festive occasions. You could make them any shape you like but, whatever you decide, you'll love that chocolate, fruit and nut combination.

Honey Crunch Creams

Joe Schreiber

Makes 20
Time: 30 minutes

For the dough
Self-raising flour   250 g/9 oz/¼ cup
Bicarbonate of soda (baking soda)
   5 ml/2 tsp
Caster sugar   50 g/2 oz/¼ cup
Unsalted butter, cold, cut into cubes
   115 g/4¼ oz/generous ½ cup
Grated zest of large orange   1
Greek honey
   115 g/4¼ oz/generous ½ cup
Chopped walnuts   25 g/1 oz/¼ cup

For the filling
Unsalted butter, very soft
   50 g/2 oz/¼ cup
Icing (confectioners') sugar, sifted
   115 g/4¼ oz/generous ½ cup
Greek honey   15 ml/1 tbsp

1 Preheat the oven to 200ºC/400ºF/gas 6/ fan oven 180ºC. Line two large baking (cookie) sheets with baking parchment.

2 To make the cookies, whisk together the flour, bicarbonate of soda and sugar. With a pastry blender or your fingertips, rub in the butter until the mixture resembles coarse breadcrumbs about the size of peas. Stir in the orange zest.

3 Gently warm the honey in a small pan over a very low heat just until it is runny (do not let it get hot). Stir it into the flour mixture and mix until combined into a firm dough.

4 Cut the dough in half and shape the first half into 20 even-sized balls. Place them well apart on the prepared baking sheets and flatten gently. Bake for about 6 minutes or until golden brown. Remove from the oven and leave for a minute or two until the cookies are firm enough to move, then transfer to a wire rack to cool completely. Re-line the baking sheets.

5 Shape the second half of the dough into 20 balls. Roll the top side only of each ball in the chopped walnuts. Set them, nut-side up, on the baking sheet and flatten gently. Bake for about 6 minutes or until golden brown. Remove and leave cool as before.

6 To make the filling, beat the butter, icing sugar and honey in a bowl until light and fluffy. Divide evenly between the bottom sides of the cookie, then top each one with a nut-coated cookie and press them together gently.

See photograph on page 33.

4 Decadent Cakes & Desserts

Regal Toffee Cake

Stephanie Bateman

Serves 12
Time: 1½ hours

For the cake
Butter, softened   175 g/6 oz/¾ cup
Soft light brown sugar
   225 g/8 oz/1 cup
Soft dark brown sugar   25 g/1 oz
Self-raising flour, sifted
   250 g/9 oz/2¼ cups
Baking powder   5 ml/1 tsp
Eggs, beaten   3
Milk   75 ml/5 tbsp
Vanilla extract   10 ml/2 tsp

For the buttercream and topping
**Clear boiled sweets, preferably orange
   and yellow**   20
Unsalted (sweet) butter, softened
   75 g/3 oz/6 tbsp
**Icing (confectioners') sugar, preferably
   unrefined**   175 g/6 oz/1 cup
Golden (light corn) syrup   15 ml/1 tbsp
Milk   10 ml/2 tsp
Desiccated (shredded) coconut
   50 g/2 oz/½ cup
Soft fresh fruit such as blueberries
   150 g/5 oz

1 Preheat the oven to 180ºC/350ºF/gas 4/ fan oven 160ºC. Line the base and sides of an 18 cm/7 in square tin with greased greaseproof (waxed) paper or baking parchment.

2 To make the cake, place all the ingredients in a large bowl and beat well for about 2 minutes until smooth and well blended. Turn the mixture into the prepared tin and smooth level with the back of a spoon. Bake for 45–55 minutes or until the cake has shrunk slightly from the sides of the tin and springs back when lightly pressed with a finger.

3 Towards the end of the cooking time (when opening the oven door will no longer make the cake sink), line a baking tray with baking parchment and arrange the clear sweets closely together on top. Put in the oven for 3–4 minutes or until they have melted.

4 Remove the cake and melted sweets. Leave the cake in the tin for 10 minutes, then turn out on to a wire rack to cool. Let the melted sweets cool on the tray.

5 To make the buttercream, put the butter in a bowl and beat for a few seconds. Sift the icing sugar over and gradually mix with the butter. Add the syrup and milk and beat until light and fluffy. Finally, beat in the coconut.

6 Spread the buttercream around the sides of the cake. Break the cooled melted sweets into long shards and arrange around the edge of the cake, then fill the middle with soft fruit such as blueberries. Finish the cake with an extravagant ribbon tied in a bow.

This lovely light sponge cake could tempt you all on its own, but topped with lashings of buttercream delicately flavoured with a touch of coconut, then spiked with shards of sugar caramel, it's completely irresistible.

Sugar-sweet Brownies

Christina Chin-Parker

Makes 12
Time: 45 minutes

For the brownies
Butter   225 g/8 oz/1 cup
Soft light brown sugar
   225 g/8 oz/1 cup
Caster (superfine) sugar
   225 g/8 oz/1 cup
Eggs   4
Vanilla extract   10 ml/2 tsp
Plain (all-purpose) flour
   175 g/6 oz/1½ cups
Baking powder   5 ml/1 tsp
Salt   2.5 ml/½ tsp
Sweet potato, peeled and finely grated
   175 g/6 oz/1½ cups

For the glaze
Icing (confectioners') sugar
   175 g/6 oz/1 cup,
   plus extra for dusting
Butter   25 g/1 oz/2 tbsp
Milk   30 ml/2 tbsp
A few strawberries to garnish (optional)

1 Preheat the oven to 180ºC/350ºF/gas 4/ fan oven 160ºC. Lightly grease a 23 x 33 cm/9 x 13 in tin and line the base with greaseproof (waxed) paper or baking parchment.

2 To make the brownies, cream the butter and sugars in a large bowl until smooth and creamy. Beat in the eggs one at a time, then stir in the vanilla.

3 Sift the flour, baking powder and salt over the mixture and gently fold in until almost mixed, then add the sweet potato and continue folding until just mixed.

4 Spoon into the prepared tin and bake for 30 minutes or until firm to the touch and a skewer inserted into the middle comes out clean. Place the tin on a wire rack and leave to cool for 10 minutes.

5 To make the glaze, sift the icing sugar into a bowl. Heat the butter and milk in a pan until just melted, pour over the icing sugar and mix together. Spoon over the hot brownie bake.

6 Leave in the tin for 10 minutes, then carefully remove. Cut into 12 squares and serve warm or cold, dusting with icing sugar just before serving. Garnish with strawberries, if liked.

Glistening with a sugar glaze and lightly dusted with icing sugar, you should try this new take on our old favourite, the brownie. You'll be surprised at just how delicious sweet potato can be in a cake.

Raspberry Choc Cheesecake

Jamieanne Hassler

Serves 8
Time: 20 minutes + setting

For the base
Oil for greasing
Butter   75 g/3 oz/⅓ cup
Plain (semi-sweet) chocolate digestive
    biscuits (graham crackers),
    crushed   175 g/6 oz

For the filling
Packet of raspberry jelly
Boiling water   150 ml/¼ pint/⅔ cups
Lemon juice   1 small
Full-fat soft cheese, at room
    temperature   350 g/12 oz/1½ cups
Caster (superfine) sugar
    100 g/4 oz/½ cup
Whipping or double (heavy) cream
    150 ml/¼ pint/⅔ cup

For the sauce
Plain chocolate   100 g/4 oz
Golden (light corn) syrup
    30 ml/2 tbsp
Orange or other liqueur   30 ml/2 tbsp

1 Lightly oil a 23 cm/9 in round, loose-bottomed cake or spring-clip tin. To make the base, melt the butter in a saucepan over a medium heat. Add the crushed biscuits, stir, then turn off the heat. Mix well, then tip into the base of the tin and firm with the back of a spoon. Chill in the fridge while making the filling.

2 Dissolve the jelly in the boiling water. Leave to cool for a few minutes, then add the lemon juice and enough cold water to make up to 300 ml/½ pint/1¼ cups. Leave in a cool place until the jelly is thick and just beginning to set.

3 Put the cheese in a bowl with the sugar and stir together until combined. Mix in the jelly with a whisk, a little at a time.

4 Whip the cream until soft peaks form, then fold into the jelly mixture. Pour and scrape into the tin, then level the top and chill in the fridge until set.

5 While the cheesecake is setting, make the sauce. Melt the chocolate, syrup and liqueur in a heatproof bowl over a pan of barely simmering water. Stir until smooth. Leave to cool at room temperature.

6 To serve, loosen the sides of the cheesecake from the tin and push up the base, or remove the sides of the spring-clip tin and slide the cheesecake on to a serving plate. Cut into slices and drizzle each with the sauce before serving.

The crunchy base perfectly complements this soft raspberry cheesecake with its melt-in-the-mouth texture. Drizzle that with a chocolate and syrup sauce with a dash of orange liqueur and you have sheer indulgence.

Nut & Pretzel Cheesecake

Christina Chin-Parker

Serves 8
Time: 1½ hours

For the base
Unsalted (sweet) butter
175 g/6 oz/¾ cup,
plus extra for greasing
Pretzels, crushed 250 g/9 oz/1½ cups
Softened peanut butter
3 heaped tbsp

For the filling
Full-fat soft cheese, at room
temperature 700 g/1½ lb/3 cups
Granulated sugar 75 g/3 oz/⅓ cup
Vanilla extract 10 ml/1 tsp
Eggs, beaten 3
Grated chocolate curls to decorate

1 Preheat the oven to 160ºC/325ºF/gas 3/ fan oven 145ºC. Lightly grease the base and sides of a 20 cm/8 in round loose-bottomed cake tin or spring-clip tin.

2 To make the base, melt the butter in a saucepan, turn off the heat and stir in the crushed pretzels. Spoon into the prepared tin, pressing down firmly with the back of a spoon. Bake for 7–8 minutes until lightly browned at the edges. Remove from the oven and turn down to 150ºC/300ºF/gas 2/fan oven 135ºC.

3 Warm the peanut butter in the saucepan (it doesn't matter if there are still a few bits of pretzels) until runny, then pour over the hot pretzel base and spread out to an even layer.

4 To make the filling, put the cheese in a bowl and beat until soft. Gradually beat in the sugar and vanilla, then add the eggs a little at a time, beating after each addition, until well mixed. Pour the filling over the peanut butter and pretzel base and smooth level.

5 Bake for 45–55 minutes or until lightly set; the centre should still wobble slightly when the tin is gently shaken. Turn off the oven and leave the door slightly open. Leave the cheesecake in the oven for 30 minutes (this helps prevent it cracking), then transfer to a wire rack to cool.

6 Chill the cheesecake for several hours, then run a knife around the side of the tin to loosen and transfer to a serving plate. Decorate with chocolate curls.

An unusual recipe that makes the best use of sweet and savoury, this delicious base is made with butter and pretzels, then topped with a layer of melted peanut butter before finishing with a soft baked cheesecake.

Sticky Toffee Puddings

Renée S Suen

Serves 8
Time: 1 hour

For the sauce
Double (heavy) cream
450 ml/¾ pint/2 cups
Soft dark brown sugar
100 g/4 oz/½ cup
Golden (light corn) syrup
50 ml/2½ tbsp
Salt a pinch

For the puddings
Stoned (pitted) dates 175 g/6 oz
Water 250 ml/8 fl oz/1 cup
Bicarbonate of soda (baking soda)
5 ml/1 tsp
Unsalted (sweet) butter, softened
50 g/2 oz/¼ cup,
plus extra for greasing
Granulated sugar
150 g/5 oz/generous ½ cup
Vanilla extract 5 ml/1 tsp
Large eggs, at room temperature 2
Plain (all-purpose) flour
150 g/5 oz/1¼ cups
Baking powder 5 ml/1 tsp
Salt a pinch
Ice-cream and wafers (optional)

1 To make the sauce, gently melt the cream, sugar, syrup and salt in a heavy-based saucepan, stirring occasionally. Bring to the boil, then simmer, stirring, for 5 minutes or until the sauce is thick and coats the back of a spoon. Turn off the heat and leave to cool for 5 minutes.

2 To make the puddings, bring the dates and water to the boil in a saucepan, then remove from the heat and stir in the bicarbonate of soda. Leave to cool completely.

3 Grease a 23 cm/9 in baking dish or eight small ramekins (custard cups). Pour in half the toffee sauce and put in the freezer to chill. Reserve the rest for serving.

4 Purée the date mixture to a smooth, thick paste. Preheat the oven to 180ºC/350ºF/gas 4/fan oven 160ºC.

5 Beat the butter, sugar and vanilla until light and fluffy. Beat in the eggs, one at a time, adding a teaspoonful of the flour with each one to prevent curdling.

6 Gently fold in half of the remaining flour, followed by the date purée, the remaining flour, the baking powder and salt.

7 Spoon into the prepared dish or ramekins. Bake for 45–50 minutes if cooking in a baking dish or 30 minutes if cooking in ramekins.

8 Remove from the oven and leave to cool slightly. Cut into portions or turn out the ramekins on to warmed serving plates and top with reheated toffee sauce. If liked, top with a scoop of good-quality ice-cream and a wafer.

Everyone's favourite treat, here the rich toffee pudding – baked with moist and luxurious dates – is smothered in a caramel sauce of melted syrup, dark brown sugar and cream to give you the ultimate little treat.

Mint Ice-cream & Fudge Sauce

Daniel Paxton-Zahra

Serves 6
Time: 20 minutes + freezing

For the ice-cream
Full-fat milk   300 ml/½ pint/1¼ cups
Egg yolks   3
Caster (superfine) sugar
   50 g/2 oz/¼ cup
Cornflour (cornstarch)   2.5 ml/½ tsp
Double (heavy) cream
   300 ml/½ pint/1¼ cups
Peppermint extract   2.5 ml/½ tsp

For the sauce
Soft light brown sugar
   75 g/3 oz/⅓ cup
Butter   40 g/1½ oz/3 tbsp
Cocoa (unsweetened chocolate)
   powder   15 ml/1 tbsp
Golden (light corn) syrup
   60 ml/4 tbsp
Double cream   150 ml/¼ pint/⅔ cup
Plain (semi-sweet) chocolate, broken
   into squares   50 g/2 oz
Sprigs of mint to decorate (optional)

1 To make the ice-cream, pour the milk into a heavy-based saucepan and bring to the boil. Meanwhile, whisk together the egg yolks, sugar and cornflour in a bowl until pale and thick. Gradually whisk in the hot milk, then pour back into the pan.

2 Cook over a low heat, stirring constantly, until thickened enough to coat the back of a spoon; do not let it boil or the mixture may curdle. Pour into a bowl, cover the surface with a piece of wet greaseproof (waxed) paper or clingfilm (plastic wrap) and leave to cool.

3 Whisk together the cream and peppermint extract until soft peaks form (if liked, you can also add a few drops of green food colouring). Fold into the cold custard until evenly blended.

4 Pour the mixture into an ice-cream maker and churn until frozen. Alternatively, pour into a shallow container and freeze for 4–5 hours, whisking 2 or 3 times during freezing to ensure an even-textured ice-cream. Allow the ice-cream to soften for about 15 minutes at room temperature before scooping and serving.

5 To make the sauce, put the sugar, butter, cocoa and syrup in a saucepan over a very low heat, stirring occasionally until the sugar has melted. Bring to the boil and simmer gently for 5 minutes.

6 Turn off the heat and add the cream and chocolate. Stir until the chocolate has melted and the sauce is smooth. Serve warm or cold, poured over scoops of the mint ice-cream. If liked, decorate each serving with a sprig of mint.

Thick, shiny and gooey, this rich fudge sauce slowly coats the peppermint ice-cream beneath, lusciously warm against fresh cold. Ice-cream is a simple treat to make, but you can always use the sauce on ready-made ice-cream or other desserts.

Mocha Brownie Puds

Meeta Wolff

Serves 4–6
Time: 45 minutes

For the brownies
Bittersweet (extra-dark) chocolate
    175 g/6 oz
Eggs   3
Caster (superfine) sugar
    150 g/5 oz/generous 1⅔ cup
Sunflower oil   90 ml/6 tbsp
Plain (all-purpose) flour
    90 g/3½ oz/scant 1 cup
Cocoa (unsweetened chocolate)
    powder   15 g/½ oz
Salt   a pinch
Espresso coffee powder
    7.5 ml/1½ tsp
Walnuts, roughly chopped
    115 g/4½ oz/generous 1 cup
Chocolate chips
    65 g/2½ oz/generous ½ cup

For the glaze
Double (heavy) cream
    150 ml/¼ pint/⅔ cup
Milk (sweet) or plain (semi-sweet)
    chocolate, roughly chopped
    150 g/5 oz
Cocoa powder   5 ml/1 tsp

1 Preheat the oven to 180ºC/350ºF/gas 4/
fan oven 160ºC. Grease an 18 cm/7 in
square tin and line the base with baking
parchment.

2 To make the brownies, break the
chocolate into squares and put in a
heatproof bowl over a pan of simmering
water. Stir occasionally until melted, then
remove from the heat and allow to cool
for a few minutes.

3 In another bowl, whisk together the eggs
and sugar until pale and thick. Drizzle
in the oil in a thin stream, whisking
continuously. Gently fold in the melted
chocolate. Sift the flour, cocoa, salt and
coffee over the mixture and fold in with
the walnuts and chocolate chips until
just mixed.

4 Spoon into the prepared tin and level the
top. Bake for 25 minutes on the middle
shelf of the oven. Transfer to a wire rack.

5 While the pudding cooks, to make the
glaze, heat the cream in a saucepan
until it is steaming hot, but not boiling.
Remove from the heat and add the
chocolate. Stir until the chocolate has
melted and the sauce is smooth.

6 Leave the sauce to cool and thicken for
10–15 minutes. When it has reached a
thick and creamy consistency, pour over
the brownie bake.

7 Cut into squares and serve barely warm,
dusted with cocoa. Alternatively, allow to
cool in the tin, then chill in the fridge for
1–2 hours before cutting.

With a thick chocolate glaze poured over wonderful mocha brownies, you can serve this little treat just warm or chill it and serve it cold. You can try cutting it into smaller pieces if you like but you know you'll want at least two!

Fruit & Lemon Pancakes

Christina Chin-Parker

Makes about 8
Time: 25 minutes

For the pancakes
Plain (all-purpose) flour
100 g/4 oz/1 cup
Salt a pinch
Egg 1
Milk 300 ml/½ pint/1¼ cups
Sunflower oil for frying

For the compôte
Soft fruit such as strawberries,
blueberries or blackcurrants
225 g/8 oz
Balsamic vinegar 5 ml/1 tsp
Caster (superfine) sugar 30 ml/2 tbsp

For the lemon butter
Unsalted (sweet) butter, softened
50 g/2 oz/¼ cup
Icing (confectioner's) sugar
60 ml/4 tbsp
Lemon juice 10 ml/2 tsp
Lemon curd 60 ml/4 tbsp

To serve
Whipped cream and icing sugar

1 To make the pancakes, sift the flour and salt into a bowl and make a hollow in the middle. Add the egg and milk to the hollow and whisk together, then gradually mix in the flour to make a smooth batter. Cover and leave to stand for 15 minutes.

2 Meanwhile, to make the fruit compôte, cut larger fruit such as strawberries in half, then put the fruit in a saucepan with the vinegar and sugar. Heat gently for 10 minutes, then transfer the fruit with a slotted spoon to a bowl and boil the juices for a few minutes until thickened. Pour over the fruit.

3 To make the lemon butter, beat the butter for a few seconds, then sift the icing sugar over and beat again for about a minute. Finally, beat in the lemon juice and lemon curd.

4 Heat a little oil in an 18 cm/7 in pancake pan or frying pan. Pour in just enough batter to thinly cover the base. Cook over a moderately high heat for about 1 minute or until golden brown underneath. Toss or turn the pancake and cook the other side for 45 seconds to 1 minute until golden.

5 Lift the pancake on to a plate, cover with a piece of greaseproof (waxed) paper and keep warm in a low oven. Repeat with the remaining batter, stacking up the cooked pancakes with greaseproof paper in between.

6 Spread a little of the lemon butter over each pancake and fold in half, then in half again. Top with a spoonful each of the fruit compôte, lemon butter and whipped cream. Dust with icing sugar before serving.

Replete with childhood memories and associations, this could be the most luxurious take ever on the humble pancake – so simple but so simply stunning, with the final spoonful of lemon butter on top to give it that sophisticated finish.

Tiramisu Slice

Rita J Lee

Serves 9
Time: 50 minutes

For the sponge
Butter, softened   175 g/6 oz/¾ cup
Caster (superfine) sugar
    175 g/6 oz/¾ cup
Eggs, beaten   3
Ground almonds   50 g/2 oz/½ cup
Self-raising flour   100 g/4 oz/1 cup
Milk   15 ml/1 tbsp

For the filling
Caster sugar   15 ml/1 tbsp
Hot espresso or very strong coffee
    60 ml/4 tbsp
Mascarpone cheese   250 g/9 oz tub
Marsala, Madeira or sweet sherry
    45 ml/3 tbsp
Icing (confectioners') sugar, sifted
    45 ml/3 tbsp
Double (heavy) cream
    150 ml/¼ pint/⅔ cup

For the topping
Icing sugar   30 ml/2 tbsp
Cocoa (unsweetened chocolate)
    powder   30–45 ml/2–3 tbsp
White chocolate curls to decorate

1   Preheat the oven to 180ºC/350ºF/
    gas 4/fan oven 160ºC. Grease and line a
    20 cm/8 in square tin.

2   For the sponge, beat the butter and
    sugar until light and fluffy. Beat in the
    eggs, a little at a time, adding a spoonful
    of ground almonds with each addition.

3   Stir in the remaining almonds, then fold
    in the flour and milk. Spoon into the tin
    and level the top.

4   Bake for 30 minutes or until well risen
    and springy to the touch. Loosen the
    edges of the sponge with a palette knife
    and leave in the tin for 10 minutes. Turn
    out, and transfer to a wire rack to cool
    completely.

5   When cold, peel off the lining and trim
    the top flat, if necessary. Cut in half
    horizontally. Line the tin with a double
    layer of clingfilm (plastic wrap) and place
    the top half of the sponge back in the
    tin. Stir the sugar into the warm coffee
    until dissolved and sprinkle half over the
    cake in the tin.

6   Put the Mascarpone in a bowl, then
    whisk in the Marsala, Madeira or sherry
    and icing sugar until blended. Whisk
    in the cream until the mixture has the
    consistency of whipped cream. Spread
    evenly over the cake.

7   Sprinkle the cut side of the cake with the
    remaining coffee mixture and place on
    top of the cream, cut-side down. Press
    down firmly.

8   To make the topping, sift the icing sugar
    over the cake in a thick, even layer, then
    sift the cocoa powder over in a thick,
    even layer. Chill in the fridge for at least
    1 hour, then carefully lift the cake out of
    the tin using the clingfilm and place on a
    serving plate.

9   Cut the cake into nine squares to serve.
    Decorate each piece with a few white
    chocolate curls.

The classic Italian dessert is here given a slightly firmer
finish that then melts so deliciously in your mouth.
Close your eyes and indulge your imagination and you'll surely
feel that Italian sunshine.

Lemon Meringue Pie

Jamieanne Hassler

Serves 6–8
Time: 1 hour

For the pastry
Butter, chilled   75 g/3 oz/6 tbsp
Plain (all-purpose) flour
   150 g/5 oz/1¼ cups
Icing (confectioners') sugar, sifted
   25 g/1 oz/scant ¼ cup,
   plus extra for dusting
Salt   a pinch
Egg yolk   1
Cold water   10 ml/2 tsp

For the filling
Cornflour (cornstarch)   30 ml/2 tbsp
Caster (superfine) sugar
   100 g/4 oz/½ cup
Lemon zest, finely grated
   2 large lemons
Lemon juice   120 ml/4 fl oz/½ cup
Water   200 ml/7 fl oz/scant 1 cup
Butter   75 g/3 oz/6 tbsp
Egg   1
Egg yolks   3

For the meringue
Egg whites, at room temperature   4
Caster sugar   225 g/8 oz/1 cup
Cornflour   10 ml/2 tsp

1 To make the pastry, cut the butter into small cubes, then rub into the flour, icing sugar and salt until the mixture resembles breadcrumbs. Mix the egg yolk and water and stir into the mixture, then gently knead on a lightly floured surface for a few seconds until smooth.

2 Flatten the pastry slightly and wrap in clingfilm (plastic wrap). Chill in the fridge for 30–45 minutes.

3 Roll out the pastry and use to line a 23 x 2.5 cm/9 x 1 in loose-bottomed flan tin (pie pan). Trim the edges. Prick the base with a fork, line with foil, shiny-side down, and chill for at least 30 minutes.

4 Put a baking (cookie) sheet in the oven and preheat to 200ºC/400ºF/gas 6/ fan oven 180ºC. Fill the foil-lined flan tin with baking beans and bake for 15 minutes, then remove the foil and beans and bake for 5 minutes. Turn the oven to 180ºC/350ºF/gas 4/fan oven 160ºC.

5 To make the filling, mix the cornflour, sugar and lemon zest in a pan, then stir in the lemon juice and water. Cook over a medium heat, stirring, until thick. Remove from the heat and stir in the butter, cut into small cubes. Beat together the egg and egg yolks and stir in.

6 To make the meringue, whisk the egg whites until soft peaks form. Add half the sugar, a spoonful at a time, whisking after each addition. Whisk in the cornflour, then add the remaining sugar as before, whisking until thick and glossy. Spoon into a piping bag fitted with a large plain nozzle (tip).

7 Return the filling to the heat and stir until it thickens and is steaming hot. Pour into the pastry case, then, starting from the edge, pipe the meringue in a pattern.

8 Bake in the oven for 20 minutes or until the top is crisp and lightly browned. Leave in the tin for 30 minutes, then remove and serve warm or cold.

A crisp, sweet shortcrust pastry is filled with a tangy lemon
layer, then topped with fluffy meringue. An all-time
classic and a much-loved dessert, this is a sophisticated little
version to inspire you, but even if yours is simpler it will taste
just as delicious.

Mini Chocolate Volcanoes

Joe Schreiber

Makes 16
Time: 1 hour

For the truffle balls
Milk (sweet) chocolate, finely chopped
  100 g/4 oz
Double (heavy) cream   60 ml/2 tbsp
Butter   7.5 g/1½ tbsp
Rum   7.5 ml/1½ tbsp

For the cakes
Plain (semi-sweet) chocolate, finely chopped   100 g/4 oz
Butter   100 g/4 oz/½ cup
Large eggs, separated   4
Granulated sugar   150 g/5 oz/⅔ cup
Natural cocoa (unsweetened chocolate) powder, sifted
  25 g/1 oz/¼ cup
Pure vanilla extract   2.5 ml/½ tsp
Ancho chilli powder   a pinch
Salt   a pinch

1 To make the truffle balls, melt the chocolate, cream, butter and rum in a heatproof bowl over a pan of gently simmering water, stirring until smooth. Remove from heat and place the bowl in the refrigerator for about 20 minutes, stirring every 5 minutes or so until the mixture becomes quite thick.

2 Scoop out 16 truffles, using a small spoon or melon baller, and place on a plate. Cover and put in the fridge until needed.

3 Preheat the oven to 150ºC/300ºF/gas 2/ fan oven 135ºC and grease or line 16 muffin tins.

4 To make the cakes, melt the chocolate and butter in a heatproof bowl over a pan of gently simmering water, stirring until melted. Remove and set aside.

5 Beat the egg yolks with half the sugar until they are thick and light and fall back from the whisk in a ribbon. Stir in the cocoa, vanilla, chilli powder and salt. Fold in the melted chocolate mixture until combined.

6 In a separate bowl, beat the egg whites until frothy. Gradually add the remaining sugar, a little at a time, until the mixture forms soft peaks. Fold two spoonfuls of this mixture gently into the cake mixture, then gently fold in the remaining egg whites, mixing as little as possible.

7 Reserve 1½ cups of the mixture and carefully divide the rest between the prepared muffin tins. Bake in the oven for 15 minutes.

8 Remove from the oven and place one cold truffle in each cake, pushing down through the crust until it is about even with the top. Cover with the reserved batter. Return to the oven for a further 20 minutes; the cakes should rise and then begin to fall back down.

9 Remove and leave to cool for about 20 minutes on a wire rack before unmoulding them.

See photograph on page 1.

5 Scrumptious Sweets

Rich Chocolate Fudge

Jamieanne Hassler

Makes 64 pieces
Time: 15 minutes

Unsalted (sweet) butter
75 g/3 oz/6 tbsp
Plain (semi-sweet) chocolate, chopped
500 g/18 oz
Can of sweetened condensed milk
400 g/14 oz/large
Vanilla extract   2.5 ml/½ tsp
Plain chocolate chips
25 g/1 oz/¼ cup

1 Line a 20 cm/8 in square tin with baking parchment.

2 Put the butter, chopped chocolate and condensed milk in a heavy-based pan. Heat gently, stirring constantly, until the chocolate and butter have melted, but do not let the mixture boil.

3 Remove from the heat and beat in the vanilla. Continue to stir for a minute or two until thickened. Pour into the prepared tin and smooth the top. Immediately sprinkle with the chocolate chips.

4 Leave to cool, then chill in the fridge for at least 1 hour or until very firm. Remove from the tin and transfer to a board. Peel off the baking parchment and cut the fudge into 2.5 cm/1 in squares.

5 Store in an airtight container at room temperature for slightly soft fudge or in the fridge for a firmer texture.

You won't believe how easy this is to make – or how often you'll sneak back to the fridge for just another tiny piece. It's very rich, utterly wicked and, if you have only a normal will power, I suggest you keep this temptation under lock and key.

Honeycomb Cinder Toffee

Louise Beall

Serves 10
Time: 20 minutes

Caster (superfine) sugar
  300 g/11 oz/1⅓ cups
Golden (light corn) syrup
  200 g/7 oz/generous ½ cup
Bicarbonate of soda (baking soda)
  2 heaped tsp

1 Line a baking (cookie) sheet with baking parchment. Put the sugar and syrup in a medium-sized heavy-based pan and stir together.

2 Put the pan over a low heat and stir gently with a wooden spoon until the sugar has melted. Turn up the heat a little and measure the temperature with a sugar (candy) thermometer. When it reaches 150ºC/300ºF, or when a teaspoonful dropped into a cup of iced water separates into hard brittle threads that snap easily, remove from the heat.

3 Add the bicarbonate of soda and stir briskly, taking care as the mixture will bubble furiously. Mix well.

4 Pour on to the lined baking sheet and leave to cool. When cold, break into pieces. Store in a single layer in an airtight container.

It's unlikely you'll need the airtight container for long as this little treat is so delicious to enjoy on your own or with friends – preferably not too many as you'll want more than one piece of this traditional little treat.

Flaked Almond Toffee

Glory Albin

Makes about 20 pieces
Time: 40 minutes

Butter   225 g/8 oz/1 cup,
   plus extra for greasing
Golden (light corn) syrup
   175 g/6 oz/½ cup
Caster (superfine) sugar
   300 g/11 oz/1⅓ cups
Vanilla extract   5ml/1 tsp
Flaked (slivered) almonds
   75 g/3 oz/¾ cup
Plain (semi-sweet) chocolate chips
   100 g/4 oz/1 cup

1 Grease a piece of foil and place it on a baking (cookie) sheet or board. Put the butter, syrup and sugar in a heavy-based pan.

2 Stir the mixture over a medium-low heat almost constantly until the temperature reaches 150ºC/300ºF on a sugar (candy) thermometer, or when a teaspoonful dropped into a cup of iced water separates into hard brittle threads that snap easily. This will take about 30 minutes; don't be tempted to turn up the heat or the toffee may spoil.

3 Remove the pan from the heat and stir in the vanilla and 50 g/2 oz/½ cup of the almonds. Pour on to the foil and spread out to about 5 mm/¼ in thick.

4 Scatter the chocolate chips evenly over the hot toffee. Leave for a minute or two until melted, then spread out in an even layer. Scatter the remaining almonds over the top.

5 Leave until the chocolate has just set, but has not completely hardened, and mark into squares. When completely cold, break up into pieces. Store in an airtight tin and eat within a week of making.

A delicate crisp of chocolate, nuts and toffee, what better indulgence to serve your guests with coffee after a wonderful meal. It takes a little time and concentration but it's worth every minute.

Shortbread & Almond Bars

Jeniffer Paxton

**Makes about 20 bars or
30 foiled-cased chocolates
Time: 1 hour**

For the shortbread
Butter, softened
150 g/5 oz/generous ⅔ cup
Caster (superfine) sugar
75 g/3 oz/⅓ cup
Plain (all-purpose) flour
150 g/5 oz/1¼ cups
Rice flour   75 g/3 oz/¾ cup
Vanilla extract   5 ml/1 tsp

For the chocolates
Plain (semi-sweet) chocolate, chopped
225 g/8 oz
**Vienna (caramel-coated) or toasted
almonds, chopped**
25 g/1 oz/¼ cup
**Gold-leaf tipped vienna or whole
blanched almonds**   20–30

1 Preheat the oven to 150ºC/300ºF/gas 2/
fan oven 135ºC.

2 To make the shortbread, beat together
the butter and sugar until light and
creamy. Sift the flours over, then stir in
with the vanilla until just mixed. Gently
knead for half a minute until smooth,
then press into a 20 cm/8 in round tin.
Use the back of a spoon to smooth and
level the surface.

3 Prick the shortbread all over with a fork,
then mark into eight equal triangular
pieces, cutting right through the dough.
Bake for 35–40 minutes or until a pale
straw colour. Remove from the oven and
leave in the tin for 5 minutes. Cut into
pieces again, then transfer to a wire rack
to cool.

4 To make the chocolates, melt 200 g/
7 oz of the chocolate in a heatproof
bowl over a pan of barely simmering
water, stirring frequently. Remove and
leave until just cool. Crumble two of the
eight shortbread slices into small pieces,
add to the chocolate with the chopped
almonds and stir well. Eat the remaining
shortbread separately.

5 Spoon the chocolate mixture into mini
bar moulds or foil chocolate cases and
leave until the chocolate has set.

6 Melt the remaining chocolate as above,
then unmould the set chocolates and
spoon the melted chocolate over,
topping each one with a whole
gold-leaf tipped Vienna almond or
blanched almond.

Little blocks of shortbread swathed in a blanket of chocolate mixed with shortbread crumbles, then topped with an almond and sparkled with a splash of gold leaf – the ultimate sophisticated indulgence.

Cinnamon-sugar Doughnuts

Glory Albin

Makes 18
Time: 30 minutes

For the doughnut cakes
Butter 90 g/3½ oz/scant ½ cup
Caster (superfine) sugar
 100 g/4 oz/½ cup
Egg, beaten 1
Plain (all-purpose) flour
 175 g/6 oz/1½ cups
Baking powder 5 ml/1 tsp
Salt a pinch
Freshly grated nutmeg 1.5 ml/¼ tsp
Vanilla extract 5 ml/1 tsp
Milk 120 ml/4 fl oz/½ cup

For the coating
Butter 90 g/3½ oz/scant ½ cup
Caster sugar 100 g/4 oz/½ cup
Ground cinnamon 10 ml/2 tsp

1 Preheat the oven to 180ºC/350ºF/gas 4/fan oven 160ºC. Lightly grease two 9-hole mini muffin tins.

2 To make the doughnut cakes, cream together the butter and sugar until light. Beat in the egg, a little at a time, beating well after each addition. Sift the flour, baking powder, salt and nutmeg into a bowl. Add a third to the creamed mixture and stir until almost mixed. Stir the vanilla into the milk, then pour half into the mixture and stir briefly.

3 Stir in half of the remaining flour mixture, followed by the rest of the milk and ending with the rest of the flour. Mix until just combined.

4 Divide the mixture between the prepared tins and bake for 12 minutes until firm. Leave in the tins for a few minutes, then turn out and transfer to a wire rack to cool.

5 To make the coating, melt the butter, then pour into a bowl. Mix together the sugar and cinnamon in another bowl.

6 Roll each doughnut cake first in the butter and then in the cinnamon sugar until thickly coated.

Made in a mini size so they are even more delicious, who can resist the softness of fresh doughnuts, and the fun of licking the cinnamon sugar off your fingers when you have finished your little treat.

Millionaire's Shortbread

Christina Chin-Parker

Makes 9 squares
Time: 40 minutes

For the base
Plain (all-purpose) flour
  175 g/6 oz/1½ cups
Caster (superfine) sugar
  50 g/2 oz/¼ cup
Chilled butter   100 g/4 oz/½ cup

For the filling
**Can of dulce de leche or sweetened
  condensed milk**   400 g/14 oz/large

For the topping
**Plain (semi-sweet) or bittersweet
  (extra-dark) chocolate, broken into
  pieces** 175 g/6 oz
Unsalted (sweet) butter   5 ml/1 tsp
**Sprigs of mint and fresh berries to
  decorate (optional)**

1 Preheat the oven to 180ºC/350ºF/gas 4/fan oven 160ºC. Lightly grease a 23 cm/9 in square loose-bottomed tin and line the base with baking parchment.

2 To make the base, mix together the flour and sugar in a bowl. Cut the butter into cubes and rub into the flour and sugar until the mixture resembles fine breadcrumbs. Knead together until it forms a dough, then press into the base of the prepared tin.

3 Prick the biscuit base all over with a fork and bake for 20 minutes or until firm to the touch and very lightly browned. Transfer to a wire rack to cool while making the filling.

4 To make the filling, if using dulce de leche, warm the caramel in a heatproof bowl over a pan of barely simmering water until smooth and pourable. If using sweetened condensed milk, pour into a heatproof bowl and place over a pan of simmering water. Cover and cook over a low heat, stirring occasionally, for 1–1½ hours or until it has turned a caramel colour. Remove from the heat and stir until smooth. Pour the caramel over the baked shortbread and leave to set.

5 To make the topping, melt the chocolate and butter in a heatproof bowl over a pan of barely simmering water, stirring occasionally. Leave to cool, then spread evenly over the caramel.

6 Leave to set at room temperature, then chill in the fridge for 15 minutes. Remove from the tin and cut into squares using a sharp knife. Store in an airtight container in a cool place or in the fridge. Serve each square garnished with a sprig of mint and fresh berries, if liked.

Another classic recipe that never goes out of style, is it the fact that you have three such delicious delicacies all in one that makes this so enduringly popular? You'll just have to try it to see if you agree.

Coconut & Choc Mint Bars

Christina Chin-Parker

Makes 9
Time: 45 minutes

For the base
Unsalted (sweet) butter
  100 g/4 oz/½ cup
Plain (semi-sweet) chocolate
  300 g/11 oz
Golden (light corn) syrup
  150 g/5 oz/scant ½ cup
Digestive biscuits (graham crackers)
  225 g/8 oz
Desiccated (shredded) coconut
  100 g/4 oz/1 cup

For the mint layer
Butter 65 g/2½ oz/scant ⅓ cup
Crème de menthe 45 ml/3 tbsp
Icing (confectioners') sugar, sifted
  350 g/12 oz/2 cups

For the topping
Butter 50 g/2 oz/¼ cup
Plain chocolate chips
  175 g/6 oz/1½ cups

1 Line an 18 x 28 cm/7 x 11 in tin, at least 6 cm/2½ in deep, with baking parchment.

2 To make the base, melt the butter, chocolate and syrup in a heatproof bowl over a pan of barely simmering water, stirring occasionally, until smooth. Remove the bowl and leave to cool for a few minutes.

3 Meanwhile, put the biscuits in a plastic bag and crush them with a rolling pin into a mixture of small pieces and crumbs.

4 Stir the crushed biscuits and coconut into the chocolate mixture. Spoon and scrape into the prepared tin and smooth the surface level. Chill in the fridge for a few minutes while making the mint layer.

5 To make the mint layer, melt the butter gently in a pan. Remove from the heat and stir in the crème de menthe. Gradually mix in the icing sugar and stir until smooth. Pour and spread over the chocolate biscuit layer. Leave to set for about an hour at room temperature.

6 To make the topping, melt together the butter and chocolate in a heatproof bowl over a pan of barely simmering water, stirring occasionally, until smooth. Pour and spread over the mint layer.

7 Chill in the fridge for 30 minutes or until the chocolate topping is firm, but not hard. Cut into 9 bars. Store in an airtight container in the fridge.

Mint and chocolate go so well together, you'll be sure to enjoy these mint bars with the texture and flavour of coconut and a dash of crème de menthe. Try them as an afternoon treat or to complete a meal.

Index